THE GREAT LATKE-HAMANTASH DEBATE

THE GREAT
LATKE
HAMANTASH
DEBATE

EDITED BY RUTH FREDMAN CERNEA
FOREWORD BY TED COHEN

THE UNIVERSITY OF CHICAGO PRESS ✡ CHICAGO AND LONDON

RUTH FREDMAN CERNEA is an anthropologist specializing in Jewish culture. She is the author of a book on Jewish ritual and symbolism, *The Passover Seder: Afikoman in Exile*, and of a forthcoming book about the Baghdadi Jewish Diaspora, *Two Promised Lands: Baghdadi Jews in British Burma*. She has served as director of research and publications for the international Hillel Foundations, and as editor of *The Hillel Guide to Jewish Life on Campus*.

The University of Chicago Press, Chicago 60637
The University of Chicago Press, Ltd., London
© 2006 by The University of Chicago
All rights reserved. Published 2006
Printed in the United States of America
15 14 13 12 11 10 09 08 07 06   1 2 3 4 5
ISBN 0-226-10023-5 (cloth)

Library of Congress Cataloging-in-Publication Data
The great latke-hamantash debate / edited by
    Ruth Fredman Cernea ; foreword by Ted Cohen.
        p. cm.
    Includes bibliographical references.
    ISBN 0-226-10023-5 (cloth : alk. paper)
    1. Jews—Humor. 2. Cookery, Jewish—Humor. I.
    Cernea, Ruth Fredman.
    PN6231.J5G66 2006
    641.5'676'0207—dc22   2005015165

♾The paper used in this publication meets the minimum requirements of the American National Standard for Information Sciences—Permanence of Paper for Printed Library Materials, ANSI Z39.48-1992.

CONTENTS

Round Six
Semiotics and Anti-Semiotics

✡ ✡ ✡

Noshes

Zalman Usiskin, Harry Harootunian, Howard Aronson,
Bernard S. Cohn, Ralph W. Nicholas
131

Round Nine
Mythdefying Origins

FOREWORD

More than twenty-five years ago, the late Rabbi Danny Leifer invited me to participate in the Latke-Hamantash Debate (my modest but commendable effort is reprinted in this collection), and then, soon after, he asked me to take a turn as moderator. In those years the moderator simply read the gag biographies the participants wrote of themselves. I prepared to do that, but when I noticed that some biographies were longer than others, I undertook to beef up the shorter ones by making serious, savage fun of the participants. This pleased the gentle Rabbi Leifer, and he next asked me to take the position of permanent moderator, which I continue to do with the generous permission and approval of Rabbi Leifer's successor, Rabbi David Rosenberg.

During my tenure as moderator I have watched the audience more than double, ever larger venues be engaged, and an amazingly broad range of faculty participate. No doubt there is much serious study to be made of why the debate has succeeded so famously, and, in particular, why it has done so well at the University of Chicago. No doubt also, this is because a debate meant to make fun of the participants themselves and their alleged professional expertise is so well suited to the University of Chicago, a wonderful place, but one that takes itself so seriously that it risks descending into a grimness unto death. But I will leave that study to others better qualified and confine myself here to one point, namely, the characteristics of the humor attempted during the debates.

First Rabbi Leifer and lately Rabbi David Rosenberg have consulted me regularly in deciding whom to invite to participate. I have done my best. The longer I've been at the university, the more people I know who are potential debaters, and I've worked hard to adhere to Rabbi Leifer's guidelines (still followed) that there must be at least one non-Jew every year, and that we include women debaters. Whatever my demographic contributions may have been worth, one thing has turned up that is of infinite value to me. It is learning that anyone is a fool who thinks he can predict what will be funny, what makes things funny, or who will be funny. Some of those we chose only as a last resort, to make up the required *minyan*, and whom we expected to fall flat, have been among our most successful debaters, leaving the audience and the rest of the panel gasping in laughter. And some of those we knew to be brilliantly witty have indeed fallen flat. Humor is a great, wonderful, indispensable gift (given by God, I like to think), and it is utterly mysterious. Those who have produced comprehensive "theories" of humor—Freud, for instance—invariably show themselves not to know a *kishke* from a *knish*. Is the word *putz* funny? Well, yes, but only sometimes. How about a line about Jewish converts to Quakerism—"Some of my best Jews are Friends"? Maybe. Maybe not. What do you think? It depends, of course. Depends on what? Only a fool would say.

The selections in this collection are well worth reading, all on their own, but there are two things which, if kept in mind, may make them even richer. First is the obvious—but easily forgotten—fact that there are many, many different forms of humor. Speakers in the great symposium indulge in almost every imaginable kind of humor, including wordplay, punning, complex storytelling, straightforward jokes, and downright vulgarity. It is a continuing amazement to me that every one of these enterprises succeeds with the audience. Not every member of the audience laughs at every effort, but virtually everything is laughed at by someone, and, just as surprising, there are members of the audience who like both very sophisticated humor and extremely vulgar jokes. When reading, ask yourself just which things you like best, and why.

Second, and less obvious, is the common background for all the lectures, namely that they are being presented by some of the most serious and accomplished academic intellectuals in the world. There is something especially amusing in hearing a Nobel laureate or university president or MacArthur Fellow making jokes while also making fun of himself and the discipline in which he works (for instance, see the contributions by Milton Friedman, Leon Lederman,

Hanna Gray, Harold Shapiro, Judith Shapiro, and Michael Silverstein).

If no one can say just what makes things funny, it is also true that no one can say just what makes Jewish humor Jewish. I would not dare to try, but I will note that an abiding characteristic of (some) Jewish humor is its relation to the Jewish proclivity for wordplay, and for intense reasoning. In many of these lectures you will find the lecturer proving, with deductive rigor, and in the arcane terminology of obscure academic disciplines, plainly insane conclusions—for instance, that Machiavelli must have been Jewish, or that their common commitment to potatoes shows that Jews and the Irish are pretty much the same.

Do you think the humanists and social scientists are funnier than the scientists and doctors? Certainly not always. Do you think that the humor must always be broad, never subtle? A few years ago Isaac Abella began his presentation by walking off stage and returning with a life-size cardboard cutout of Einstein, which he proceeded to stand near him at the lectern, and about which he never said one word. It was a smash. The audience understood the whole thing almost immediately, and the longer Isaac went on ignoring his celebrated companion, the funnier it seemed. Here was a distinguished physicist attempting to articulate a general theory that would explain latkes, hamantashen, and much more—a theory that he called "GUT" on the model of the desired Grand Unified Theory of contemporary physics. In an attempt to add weight and authority to his presentation he was invoking his relationship to the greatest physicist of all, namely Einstein (a Jew, of course), and he left it to the audience to understand this as his point in bringing out the Einstein effigy. At first, I was astonished by this subtlety, and then was delighted to watch the audience grasp it.

Which brings us to the audience. It is motley, but there are a few identifiable cadres. There are the Hillel people, always, those who make a point of attending Hillel events, including this one. Then there are University of Chicago students in general, especially ones attracted in a given year because they've studied with one of the debaters. And there is also a significant group of people who have no connection either with Hillel or with the university, but who just seem to like this affair and come to it every year. Some of this last group come from many miles away. If we can't say exactly what's funny about the things that are funny, even less can we say just what this audience gets for its money (in fact admission is free), and my guess is that different audience members get different things. Some like the wit, some like the scatology, some like the display (we now have costumes), and some seem just to like the idea of the whole thing.

A participant in the debate, if he has a reflective soul, might well wonder just how he strikes the audience. Of course the speaker is trying to make them laugh, but how do they regard the speaker—as an amateur stand-up comic, as a satirist, as a good-natured fellow willing to make a fool of himself? Or—and let us finally get to this—as a Jew? I forgot to mention that many audience members are not Jewish. I sometimes wonder if they are reading Jewishness into some of the proceedings, while the Jewish part of the audience sees things differently. Are Jews smart, witty, funny, clever, show-offy, egotistical, self-important—or what? Which Jews? In fact I don't know how clear the audience is about which of the debaters are Jews and which not (remember that we always have at least one non-Jew on the panel, and sometimes even more). It is occasionally unmistakable, as it was a few years ago when Barbara Stafford participated and began by informing the audience that she'd been invited as a *Talmudus ignoramus*. But even then, the non-Jews are as likely as the Jews to sprinkle in Yiddish expressions and refer to Jewish icons. So what is going on?

The University of Chicago is a peculiar institution. It is a great place and a peer among America's and the world's great universities, but it carries on its work with far fewer resources than other places. It has a byzantine administrative structure unlike that of any other university I know. It is academically very conservative, and yet it sponsors interdisciplinary work at an extraordinary level. And within the university there is this annual debate, itself one of the most peculiar things that occur here. It is at least as well attended, every year, as almost any of the concerts, recitals, lectures, symposiums, and exhibitions that crowd the academic calendar, and while those are one-time affairs, this happens *every year*. Its success is as mysterious as the funniness itself, and surely I cannot explain it, nor am I fool enough to try. I invite you to think about it for yourself.

If you can attend a debate or two, pay attention to the audience as well as to the debaters, but a very lively sense of things can also be appreciated from the sample presentations in this collection. Think of yourself as reading a lecture, something prepared to be delivered aloud, in person, but also available in print. Remember to think of the text as first meant for a live audience, and, while you are reading, use your imagination to think of yourself as one of about a thousand auditors. Some of these lectures will surely please you, maybe make you laugh out loud. Others, perhaps, will not. And why is that?

Here is one guess about a general awareness among Jews creating a background for much of the humor. You know, of course, of Jews for whom virtually everything that happens is understood in terms of its implication for the Jews: everything is either good for the Jews or bad for the Jews; and this sometimes reaches absurd extremes when something utterly irrelevant to the Jews is appraised in this way. In these symposium lectures almost every conceivable academic enterprise is understood in this way, including atomic physics, sociology, metaphysics, aesthetics, linguistics, art history, political science, economics, and on and on. That in itself has a comical aspect, and it also has the unspoken satirical aim of making fun of the idea that the world revolves around its Jewish inhabitants. It doesn't, really, does it?

ACKNOWLEDGMENTS

All of us who build on the creativity and hard work of others are inherently in their debt, and this is especially so when writing about the Latke-Hamantash Debate. This book is itself an acknowledgment of the continuing efforts and self-reflexive good humor of American faculty for close to sixty years. The authors of the debate, anthropologist Sol Tax, historian Louis Gottshalk, and Hillel director Rabbi Maurice Pekarsky, could not, of course, foresee that they were starting a tradition, but their social insight did just that, to the delight of generations of faculty and students. The Hillel directors at the University of Chicago who followed Rabbi Pekarsky are also owed a large measure of appreciation, because without their enthusiasm and their dogged encouragement, it is doubtful that busy faculty, ever reaching for another serious academic publication, would have committed themselves year after year to writing academic spoofs. These same Hillel directors recognized the value of the event by maintaining the archives that permitted this very book.

Three individuals, three Hillel directors, who inherited the debate must be especially acknowledged and thanked. Even today, Rabbi Max Ticktin's face evidences his utter delight when he recalls his days at Chicago during the period when the debate overflowed the Hillel House and was moved to a stately building of the university. A serious scholar himself, and a renowned lecturer in Jewish history and tradition both at George Washington University and in the general community, Rabbi Ticktin took the debate with him when he went to GWU, where it continues to flourish under his loving watch. I greatly appreciate Max's encouragement, his recollections, and his generous assistance.

Invaluable to the Latke-Hamantash Debate, and profoundly appreciated, is Rabbi Daniel Leifer, who succeeded Max Ticktin as Chicago's Hillel director. Danny guided the debate for twenty-five years until his untimely death in 1996. Danny's ingenious, convoluted, improbable displays of Gematria (using numerical equivalents of the Hebrew letters to uncover hidden meanings in the text) that "illuminated" his introductions to the debate are legendary. Danny, along with assistant Hillel director Suzanne Griffel, generously opened the Latke-Hamantash archives to me and thus made this project possible. Danny's passion for the debate was infectious; for a quarter of a century, Danny was its soul, and his premature death has left a lasting void.

Danny's successor at Hillel, Rabbi David Rosenberg, gracefully and ably stepped into the breach, honoring his predecessor and continuing the tradition until this day. David's reflections as one new to Chicago and as the person now responsible for the debate's continuation, as well as his practical assistance, are greatly appreciated.

I am also deeply indebted to sociologist, gadfly, and Latke-Hamantash participant Elihu Katz, of Hebrew University/Annenberg School of Communications at the University of Pennsylvania, who has sustained his enthusiasm for the debate and has been exceptionally helpful during the past few years. I appreciate the friendship and wisdom of Israeli folklorist Dov Noy, who first identified the social importance of the debate within the context of Jewish academic life in America and within the body of American Jewish folklore, and urged me to write about it. Much appreciation is also due Harold Wechsler, whose knowledge of college selectivity patterns as they affected Jewish students and faculty helped to clarify the social situation at Chicago during the early years of the debate. Thank you to the scores of Chicago Hillel students who retyped the rough manuscripts into workable texts. I am profoundly grateful for Carol Saller's invaluable assistance in preparing the manuscript. And certainly not least though last, I happily acknowledge another sociologist-gadfly, my husband Michael Cernea, for his continuing and caring encouragement.

INTRODUCTION

In honor of the joyous holiday of Hanukkah, I should like to discuss the Book of Esther and its relevancy for us tonight. Parenthetically, I might note that the only thing that appears to be universally acknowledged as relevant today is the relevancy of demonstrating the relevancy of something which we know, deep down inside, to be totally irrelevant. At any rate, making the irrelevant relevant is an ability that is firmly ingrained in the Jewish tradition.
HOWARD I. ARONSON, University of Chicago, 1969

Absurd, celebratory, very funny, and deeply serious: this is the Latke-Hamantash Debate, born on a cold and windy day in Chicago some sixty years ago. Since then, it has traveled from the intimate space of the Hillel House at the University of Chicago to campuses nationwide, revealing the wry humor and creativity of a who's who of American faculty and acting as a carnival mirror for scores of students. In it they see a more approachable side of their sedate faculty, and can learn to laugh at their own anxieties about the seriousness of academic achievement. As eminent Israeli folklorist Dov Noy has observed, in its originality and as an indigenous popular social expression, the debate, or symposium, is a unique contribution to American folklore.

Nell Pekarsky recalled how her husband, Hillel director Rabbi Maurice Pekarsky, came home one winter day in 1946 flushed with cold and excitement, eager to tell her about the street corner meeting he just had in Hyde Park with anthropologist Sol Tax and historian Louis Gottshalk.[1] All were worried about the chill atmosphere at Chicago for Jewish faculty and students, and knew something had to be done. More significant than the weather was the alien climate of the university, especially with the approach of Christmas and its choral music, parties, and pageants. With few occasions for casual student-faculty interaction and high pressure for intellectual achievement, young Jewish students felt uncomfortable and often lonely at the university.

The brilliant idea? A Hanukkah "debate" between Jewish faculty members contesting the merits of two foods very familiar to their students, the Hanukkah latke or potato pancake, and the Purim hamantash, a filled tricornered pastry. It would be held in the warmth of a home—the Hillel House on campus, and of course there would be food: latkes, applesauce, and sour cream for the "jury." Sol Tax would be latke master chef.

The debate would also engage another group on campus that was of serious concern to Rabbi Pekarsky: the Jewish faculty. Immediately after the war, Jews were just beginning to venture far from the urban universities in the East, and Jewish identity itself was a problematic ingredient in the quest for acceptance in the scholarly world. Faculty often felt it necessary, wise, or agreeable to submerge their Jewish identities while achieving—and demonstrating—scientific objectivity and universality: intellectual achievement meant denying, divorcing, or forgetting ethnic origins. In addition, the academy's rational, objective, "scientific" approach questioned traditional teachings and practices. In another era, faculty members might have become Talmudic scholars; these days, although many were familiar with Jewish intellectual thought and religious-ethnic tradition, the new sociologists, anthropologists, lawyers, economists, scientists, and their colleagues immersed themselves in the compelling, encompassing secular university culture, one that apparently superseded the more insulated Jewish tradition they knew well. Ethnic identity went underground as the Jewish academic became universal man. Jewish students at schools of higher education rarely met Jewishly visible faculty. Faculty might be "ethnic" in their homes and hearts, but on campus, interaction with students was confined to scholarship.

Jewish faculty then lived in two distinct houses: the rational public campus and the affective, hidden childhood, their private home. The informal event created by Pekarsky, Tax, and Gottshalk in 1946 gave underground Jews a safe context in which to integrate these homes: to talk knowledgeably, if jokingly, about Jewish cultural life;

to speak the private language, Yiddish, among friends; and to display publicly their pleasure at the unsophisticated foods and traditions that satisfied their souls.

Of course, given that this is Jewish tradition, there is another "origin myth" about the Latke-Hamantash contest, this one concerning a version held only within the closed circle of graduate students. Sociologist Daniel Bell recalls:

A number of us—including Daniel Boorstin, Benjamin Nelson and Henry Finch (a philosopher who, with Edward Shils, translated Max Weber's Methodology*) —had begun a study group with Rabbi Pekarsky. Discussing the symbolism of Jewish holidays before Purim, I proposed the idea of the debate. Henry Finch and I were the two protagonists and antagonists. I say protagonists and antagonists because each debater had to take* both *sides of the argument. After all, it is easy to argue one or the other. The real test of* pilpul *("pepper"; i.e., fine argument) is to present the case for both sides. I do not recall Finch's arguments . . . I do recall mine:*

The latke ties heaven and earth. It is round, and therefore has a oneness. As one says: "Shema Yisrael, hashem elokenu, hashem echad," *("Hear O Israel, the Lord our God, the Lord is One") emphasizing the oneness. But a latke is made from potatoes. And when you eat it, it sinks straight down to the earth,* adomah. *Thus it fulfills all the conditions of our existence.*

The hamantash? The hamantash is made like a tricorn. A trinity? But God will not betray us. He gave us two *hands—not one, or three, but two. Why two? So that we can take two hamantashen to eat. And what do you have if you place one hamantash over the other—the Star of David, or the* magen david *of the* Yiddish folk, und es geht zum mogen *(and it also goes straight down to the stomach).*[2]

What was started by Pekarsky, Gottshalk, and Tax as a way of reaching out to faculty and students through a casual, intimate gathering eventually became so popular that it outgrew the confines of the Hillel House. In 1965, Hillel director Max Ticktin noted that "we had twice as many people at this program as we had at both of our Kol Nidre programs together, that is about 700 people as compared to 350 for the two services."[3] Today at Chicago this apparently eternal argument is celebrated each Tuesday before Thanksgiving in a spacious ivy-covered hall on campus, fully part of university culture, listed on the university's Web site, and a must-do for its students, whether Jewish or not. The significance of this grave topic is underscored by the formal march into the hall, complete with banners (one for the latke, one for the hamantash), "Pomp and Circumstance," and academic costumes. For close to a quarter of a century, the moderator of this august gathering has been professor of philosophy Ted Cohen, whose puns, jokes, and accrued wisdom have kept the impassioned contestants in line. Presentations follow rigorous guidelines consistent with the intellectual standing of the university: all participants must hold a PhD or equivalent degree; arguments should be framed according to the theoretical position and jargon of the participant's academic discipline; and each symposium must include someone who is not Jewish—to lend a note of "gentility."[4] Of course, like academics anywhere, participants have sometimes felt intellectually compelled to ignore the topic of the debate in order to assert their own, more exquisite argument in favor of—not the latke or hamantash—but the bagel, the herring, the *knish*, or chicken soup. Little by little, such fervent displays of academic freedom have transformed the contest from a debate to a symposium, where sides are not so strictly drawn and all manner of "proof" is presented, unchallenged.

Demonstrating their commitment to the intellectual positions posited, professors have on occasion underscored their arguments by appropriate dress: philosopher Martha Nussbaum assumed Greek costume to deliver her oration, "Euripides' *The Cooks of Troy*: Hecuba's Lament"; sociologist Daniel Levine showed up as a samurai; and Law School professor Richard Epstein—rejecting the dyadic argument and adding to the confusion by defending the *knish*—removed his outer shirt to reveal evidence of his hidden tendencies, the tie-dyed shirt lying beneath. Similarly, titles of symposia and of the talks reflect the seriousness of the undertaking, as exemplified in this title: "The Hamantash in Modernism and Postmodernism: The Effects of Deconstruction of Fabulism on the Mediation of Reader, Audience, and the World: The Text, Context, and Metatext in Pedagogy and Neopedagogy: A Retrospective Aesthetic" (Jean Peck, Cincinnati, 1990). Important issues frame the debates: "Which Has Done More to Save the Jewish People: The Latke or the Hamantash?" (Chicago, 1976); and "The First Annual International Conference on Peaceful Uses of the Latke and the Hamantash" (Chicago, 1960). Where else could promising scholars comprehend the world anew, and see that India, and the Roman Empire, are shaped like a hamantash (George Stigler, 1974; Bernard Silberman, 1979), and that Puerto Rico—and the universe!—look like latkes (Sol Tax; Morrel Cohen, 1967)? Through the years, slides, blackboards, and PowerPoint presentations have added substance to persuasive arguments such as these. As a headline in the *Chicago Tribune* proclaimed, "At the U. of C., publish or perish becomes: Pancake or pastry?"[5]

The satirists are themselves satirized through the exalted, faux credentials with which they are introduced. Bernard Weisberger's playful introduction (1962) for political scientist Hans Morgenthau is more accurate than most:

An expert on the law of nations
Now enters these deliberations
His works are read by those in power
From Nkrumah to Adenauer
And statesmen his advice are seekin'
From Nizhni Novgorod to Pekin.
His major analytic talents
He now will throw into the balance.
Twixt hamantash and latke fans
He'll let you know just where he stands.

All this is "high seriousness," explained Rabbi Daniel Leifer, the Hillel director who shepherded the event for more than two decades, as well as a satire of the academic experience: "Where the pressures for academic excellence, for research and publication, for creation of new knowledge are at their highest, there the chance to 'take a night off' and play a joke about one's daily lot and ultimate destiny is most needed, appreciated, and relished."[6] He continued:

What a stroke of genius it was for Rabbi Maurice Pekarsky to combine the Jewish tradition of intellectual parody with the tradition of academic scholarship of the secular university and to give the task of parody to the Jewish practitioners of the new forms of "Talmudic learning." Who better was there to engage in the comic critique of the secular-universal traditions of the Uni-

versity of Western Civilization than those metamorphosized Talmudic schol-
ars so recently admitted to the genteel halls of academe? For by satirizing the
institution and its enterprise, into whose halls they had striven so hard to
enter and to be accepted, these Jewish professors affirmed their separate ethnic-
cultural identities. To engage in parody, satire and comic relief is to stand
somewhat apart, on the periphery looking in; it presupposes a measure of dis-
tance and disengagement. This stance well suits the Jewish intellectual in
Western society and characterizes at least the first generations of Jewish pro-
fessors in the groves of academe. Indeed, the early Latke-Hamantash Debates
were characterized by more extensive use of Yiddish and Jewish ethnic ref-
erences than they are today.

As Rabbi Leifer suggests, it is doubtful that many people today
would immediately catch the references as well as the humor of
Bernard Weisberger's 1961 homage to the legendary Indian "Hia-
latke, good life-bringer," which plays on the Hebrew words *chai*,
"life," and *mechiah*, literally, "that which brings life," and is commonly used as the Yiddish expression for "pleasure." The earlier papers are dense with biblical, Talmudic, or linguistic references to
Jewish tradition, an in-group jargon that signified both the idea and
the experience behind it. Yiddish expressions and Yiddish inflec-
tions were understood immediately, no glossary needed. As time has
passed, this jargon is used less and less, a word here and there, a
reference to "gastronomic Judaism" (common Jewish foods such as
latkes, hamantashen, or chicken soup), as fewer presenters and
members of the audience are intimately familiar with an ethnically
Jewish lifestyle. This road so heavily traveled can be seen in the references to popular music and television, Rocky and Bullwinkle, in
the essay by William Meadow in this collection.

As parody, the debate would seem more suitable for the Jewish
early spring holiday of Purim, when masking, drinking, and parody are traditional. Indeed, parody of Jewish texts and parody as a
literary form date back to the Talmud, and have been associated with
Purim especially since the Middle Ages. But a bit of hilarity and
lightness was needed at Chicago as the winter darkness approached,
not as the spring warmth was coming to the city, not just for Jewish students but apparently for the campus as a whole. The debate
is an academic "carnival," suggests Rabbi David Rosenberg, the cur-

rent Hillel director at the University of Chicago, in that it turns the usual academic posture upside-down. Placed just before winter finals, it allows the university to make fun of itself, to release some of the tension that has been building all fall.

Since its very beginning, the debate has resonated with faculty and students at campuses throughout the United States. It has been replicated at universities such as Wisconsin, Michigan, Princeton, Yale, Penn, Bryn Mawr, Brandeis, Cornell, Los Angeles Valley College, Cincinnati, Rochester, the City College of New York, Kent State, Mount Holyoke, Rutgers, Indiana, and George Washington University. But Chicago's tradition is unique: only here has the event continued uninterrupted since 1946, and only at Chicago is the archive of presentations so carefully maintained. While on most other campuses, the debate is exclusively a Hillel event, the audience that fills Ida Noyes Hall or Mandel Hall may not even be aware of Hillel's sponsorship. Organizing the debate is a challenge; it takes great effort by the Hillel director to encourage faculty to devote precious "publish or perish" time to construct an erudite and funny paper. Still, it is an honor to be asked, and year after year, the roster of presenters is complete.

What began almost as a joke, a response to a need of the time, has flourished at the University of Chicago for well more than a half century despite numerous changes in the social atmosphere of the university and in America itself. It is no longer necessary to hide one's ethnic heritage, for Jews or other ethnic groups. Rather, assimilation and acculturation—the blending of Jewish and American identities, not the denial of one or the other—challenge a clear and defined Jewish identity. Staged in a central Gothic building, open to all students, faculty, and alumni, the apparently private ethnic event becomes a public, academic celebration, and in doing so proclaims that Jews have a rightful, natural, expected place on campus. The outsider is now in, and the outsiders' ultimate in-group event is now the emblem of Jewish integration at the university. The tentative, uncomfortable Jewish faculty and students of 1946 have come a long, long way.

Today, however, relatively fewer Jewish students come to campus schooled in the intellectual, linguistic, and even gastronomic traditions so familiar to the originators of the debate. With few strong, scholarly Jewish role models in their lives, it may be that these students find in the faculty presentations a reaffirmation of the intellectual tradition of Judaism, as well as a mode of relating to Judaism as a positive, enjoyable, comfortable, nonexclusive experience compatible with their socially integrated lives. They bring their non-Jewish fiancés and friends: many of the men I have met at these events were accompanying Jewish women friends, and a Jewish woman from New York said about her five non-Jewish classmates eating hamantashen, "I have to educate these guys!" These days, when the audience gathers after the debate to eat latkes and hamantashen, they are entertained by the a cappella group Chicago Rhythm and Jews, many of whom are not Jewish. If, in the early days, the Hillel House was a cocoon protecting Jewish students from an uncomfortable outside world, today the large university hall seems to be a mixing bowl.

Given its history, it would seem surprising that students who are not Jewish have always been a large proportion of the audience for the debate. Surely they have not been coming to proclaim the rightful place of Jews on campus. Why, then, are they here?

The University of Chicago has always attracted very bright students, many from the Midwest, who have rarely encountered Jews before coming to campus. At the same time, Jews from the East have found Chicago a happy haven: although in the 1930s, the University of Chicago imposed quotas on Jewish enrollment and faculty advancement, these quotas were never as stringent as they were at the selective schools in the East. After the Second World War, these restrictions were relaxed still further, and during the fifties and sixties, while the eastern Ivies were still tightly limiting Jewish enrollment, Jewish students constituted approximately twenty-five percent of Chicago's student body, and there were hundreds of Jewish faculty. Or more, it seemed, to non-Jewish students. Jews seemed to set the academic tone of the campus and, as one alum from Arkansas told me, it seemed as logical to learn about Jews as to learn about other aspects of the university. The debate was part of the campus culture, especially since it featured faculty who seemed distant in class. This same combination of curiosity, university culture, and need for relaxation continues to bring students of all backgrounds to the hallowed halls.

The presence at the debate of large numbers of students who are not Jewish also suggests that the experience of coping with the ethnic-universalist dilemma is a common feature of American life, especially when first-generation ethnic students reach the realms of the elite American universities. It also points to the degree of integration, or interdating and intermarriage, currently occurring in the United States. Today, it is not only Jews who are familiar with latkes, bagels, and chicken soup. Nor are other supposedly ethnic foods exclusive: tacos, chili, sushi, pizza, egg rolls, spring rolls, cappuccinos, French bread, and French fries are all handy metaphors for the ethnic American continuum.

This book, then, will give a taste of the intellectual creativity and just plain playfulness that started many years ago in a much different American world and have continued to flourish and nourish generations of students and scores of faculty at Chicago and on many other campuses.

The essays that follow have been selected from the extensive collection of papers and introductory notes that have been carefully preserved by the University of Chicago Hillel, as well as by individuals on other campuses. As presentation, many papers depended on sight gags and performance, and perhaps also on the shock, as it were, of seeing one's stolid professor joke about his or her hallowed subject. Fond memories of debates gone by often rest on such ephemeral moments, which text alone cannot restore. But time's distillation confers another advantage. In the written form, the cleverness of the arguments shines through, and the fun is embedded in a twist of logic, a play on words, a rationally absurd discussion, or a convoluted history of the place of Jewish foods in the history of Western civilization. The achievements of our famous professors on this night of all nights are all the more to be appreciated as scholarly (well, sort of) writing, long after the applause has died down.

Notes

1. Personal conversation with Nell Pekarsky, Chicago, 1995.
2. Daniel Bell, "In the Beginning," Letter to the Editor, *New Leader*, July 14–28, 1997, 23.
3. Letter to Rabbi Benjamin M. Kahn, December 2, 1965.
4. This inclusion, this "tokenism," is an ironic reversal of the tokenism that often governed Jewish faculty appointments during this period.
5. Steve Johnson, *Chicago Tribune*, November 28, 1991.
6. Rabbi Daniel Leifer, "The Great Debate: The Latke vs. the Hamantash," *Chicago Jewish Historical Society News*, December 1980, 8–12.

FOOD FOR ACADEMIC AND GASTRIC DIGESTION

Lights, Latkes, and Miracles

At the darkest time of the year, when the days are short and the moonlight absent, Jews the world over celebrate the Jewish Festival of Lights. In commemorating the Jewish victory over the Syrian Greeks in 165 BCE through the lighting of candles and oil lamps, Hanukkah not only recalls a historic event but also conveys a change of spirit, a realization of hope in despair, and the link between God and humanity through his symbols, fire and light.

As told in the two books of the Maccabees, the last books of the Apocrypha, the Syrian Greeks forbade the Jews from practicing their religion, and desecrated the holy temple. On the twenty-fifth of the Jewish month of Kislev, Judah Maccabee and his brothers led the Jews to victory, ending a conflict that had torn the country apart. Immediately, the Jews moved to restore and rededicate the temple by rekindling the essential Jewish symbol, the seven-branched *menorah*. Inside the building they found only one cruse of undefiled, consecrated olive oil with the seal of the high priest still intact; this would be sufficient for only one day. To their great surprise, the oil miraculously burned not for one but for eight days, throughout the time it took to produce more of the sanctified oil.

At Hanukkah ("dedication"), the miracles that saved the Jews throughout the ages are recounted through song, story, and action. To recall the miracle of the oil that lasted eight days, a special candelabrum with eight places for olive oil or candles is lit at dusk. The Hanukkah lamp must have eight places for the lights, all on the same level, recalling the eight nights that the *menorah* burned when the temple was rededicated. An additional place, either higher or lower, is for the *shamesh*, or "service candle," which is used to light the others. Candles (or the oil) are placed in the Hanukkah lamp from right to left—an additional one added each evening—and lit from left to right, until all lights burn brightly on the eighth night. Oil or candles must be sufficient to burn at least a half hour. Ideally, the Hanukkah lamp is placed in a window or on the left side of the doorway to shine out into the night.

On the first night, three blessings are said before lighting the candles or oil. After the first night, only the first two blessings are said.

Baruch atah Adonai, Eloheynu, melech ha-olam, asher kid'shanu b'mitzvotav vitzivanu l'hadlik ner shel Hanukkah. (Praised are You, Ado-nai our God, Sovereign of the Universe, who has made us holy by *mitzvot* and instructed us to kindle the Hanukkah lights.)

Baruch atah Adonai, Eloheynu, melech ha-olam sheh asah nissim l'avotaynu ba-yamim ha-heym bazman hazeh. (Praised are You, Ado-nai our God, Sovereign of the Universe, who performed miracles for our ancestors at this season in ancient times.)

Baruch atah Adonai, Eloheynu, melech ha-olam, sheh-hecheyanu, v'ki'manu, v'higianu lazman hazeh. (Praised are You, Ado-nai our God, Sovereign of the Universe, who has given us life, sustained us, and helped us to reach this day.)

In keeping with its nonsacred but happy connotations, Hanukkah lamps and *dreidels* have become objects of artistic creation or necessary improvisation throughout the centuries. In Yemen, Jews made stone Hanukkah lamps; in Europe the lamps were of brass, silver, or even base metal, especially during the Holocaust years; in America the Hanukkah lamp may be of glass, Lucite, metals, pottery, and such. In the blackest periods of Jewish history, hollowed-out potatoes held the candles.

It is customary on Hanukkah to "play *dreidel*"—to spin the four-sided top with the Hebrew characters *nun, gimmel, hay, sh'in,* signifying *Ness gadol haya sham,* "A great miracle happened there." A gambling game, with nuts, raisins, or small coins as currency, playing *dreidel* is similar to informal gambling games common in Europe. In Yiddish, the letters have a more practical meaning than in Hebrew: *nun* stands for "nothing"; *ganz* (*gimmel*), "everything"; *halb* (*hay*), "half"; and *shtell-arein* (*shin*), "put some in." Players place an equal number of nuts in the pot and take turns spinning the *dreidel*. If *nun* comes up, nothing happens; if *ganz*, the spinner takes everything; if *halb*, the spinner takes half; if *shtell-arein*, the number agreed on beforehand is added. Players drop out as they become bankrupt, and the winner stands alone.

Other Hanukkah traditions include giving children small amounts of money (Hanukkah *gelt*), giving larger amounts to charity, and eating cheese dishes. Eating cheese recalls a legend from the Apocrypha, that of Judith who killed the Assyrian general Holofernes by feeding him cheese and wine, and then cutting off his head while he drowsed. For this heroic act, women are said to have a special relationship to Hanukkah in addition to cooking the latkes. Hannah, the mother of the prophet Samuel, is also honored because of her great devotion to Jewish ideals. Grieving because she was long childless, Hannah vowed that if a son were born to her, she would dedicate him to the service of God. When her prayers were answered, she brought Samuel to the temple to be raised. Accordingly, pleasurable customs involving women developed in many countries, such as partying, gift-giving, or a special night in the synagogue.

Hanukkah is considered a minor holiday in the Jewish ritual cycle, but has become more prominent in recent years because of its calendrical proximity to Christmas and other winter solstice celebrations. In addition, while Jewish thought has traditionally downplayed the military aspects of the Hanukkah story in favor of religious interpretations, after the Holocaust, Hanukkah's message of military strength to preserve Jewish heritage and survival has increasing resonance.

Oil, fire—and latkes. Because oil is a key concept of Hanukkah, foods fried in oil have become traditional during the holiday. Jews of Eastern European heritage make latkes, potato (or cheese) pancakes, while in Israel, with its very diverse Jewish population, another oil-fried food, sugar-covered filled doughnuts, *sufganiyot*, are eaten.

Purim, Parody, and Pastries

Purim ("lots") is a sweet and happy time in the Jewish calendar, a time of carnival, masquerade, feasting, and an exchange of sweet foods among family and friends. Coming as it does just as spring is approaching, Purim's themes echo nature's revitalization, and suggest the movement from darkness and despair to sunshine and laughter.

Like Hanukkah, Purim commemorates a victory over oppression, but one based more in legend, metaphor, and local custom than in fact. As recounted in the Megillah, the Scroll of Esther read each year at Purim, long ago in Persia, in the town of Shushan, King Ahasuerus's evil minister Haman became incensed when Mordecai, a Jew, refused to bow down to him. Haman decided to kill all the Jews, and cast lots—*purim*, in Hebrew—to determine the day most propitious for the annihilation. The fourteenth day of the Jewish month of Adar was selected. Unknown to Haman, however, the king's favorite wife was Mordecai's niece, the beautiful Jewish Queen Esther. She had become queen after the defiant Queen Vashti refused Ahasuerus's orders to display herself before his drunken guests, thus earning Vashti a special place in the pantheon of early feminists. The massacre was averted when Esther prepared a feast for the king, plied him with wine, and successfully pleaded with him to save her life, and the lives of all the Jews. Haman was hanged on the gallows built to hang Mordecai, and the Jews have been celebrating ever since. Haman has become a prototype of all tyrants who wish to destroy the Jews, and Purim a continuing tale of the downfall of the wicked and the vindication of the innocent.

Purim, therefore, is a time of thankfulness, and as at Hanukkah, the *Sheheheyanu* prayer is recited, thanking God "who has granted us life, sustained us, and brought us to this season." Gifts are given to the needy, and *shaloch manos*, trays of fruits, pastries, nuts, and candy, are sent throughout the community, linking individuals in a dense, sweet web. Purim is one of only two times that Jewish ritual allows drinking to excess (the other is the celebration of another liberation, from Egypt, at Passover); Jews are to drink until they cannot differentiate between "Cursed be Haman" and "Blessed be Mordecai." The excessive use of wine at Purim is explained as recalling the excessive drinking by King Ahasuerus that led to Esther's becoming the queen and to overturning Haman's harsh decree.

The festival of Purim thus celebrates the world turned upsidedown: the victims become the victors, the day of death becomes the day of celebration, usually controlled drinking becomes excessive, masks hide real faces, and the would-be tyrant is obliterated: a name is understood to evoke the essence of an individual, and so each time the Megillah is read, Haman's name is drowned out, erased, by his intended victims, who stamp their feet and raucously twirl loud noisemakers, *groggers*. As winter turns into spring, cold into warm, and darkness to light, Purim is an interlude of social and ideological reversal, the Jewish "carnival." Well-chosen words also contribute to the carnival. Throughout the years *Purimspiel*, Purim parody—creating clever arguments that poke fun at traditional ways of life—became another way of mocking the status quo. The Latke-Hamantash Debate is in this tradition.

Unlike the Torah scroll, the Megillah is neither sacred nor unalterable, and through the ages artists have enhanced the Scroll of Esther with flowers, bright colors, and beautiful drawings. The Megillah case, like the Torah cases in Sephardic countries, has been crafted of finely wrought and elaborated silver or wood.

And the three-cornered hamantashen that arouse such passions in the Great Debate? These filled pastries, traditional among Jews of Eastern European heritage, are said to symbolize Haman's hat or Haman's pocket, since *tasche* means "pocket" in Yiddish and German. The pockets may be filled with a variety of sweets, but poppy seed (*mohn*) and prune jam (*lekvar*) are the most traditional. Sephardic Jews also serve a sweet pastry at this time, Haman's Ears, deep-fried strips of dough dipped in sugar syrup.

THE GREAT LATKE-HAMANTASH DEBATE

Round One

Metahamantashen, or Shooting Off the Can(n)on

Freedom, Latkes, and American Letters: An Original Contribution to Knowledge

BERNARD A. WEISBERGER

I regret that the ridiculously brief time allowed to me does not permit me to do full justice to the noble dish in whose cause I rise to speak. I promise, however, that my remarks will, like latkes, be well-rounded, though not flat. I am sorry that not everyone on this platform can say the same.

I wish to point out to you a close association between the latke and American culture, and specifically, American democracy as expressed in our literature. This linkage has long existed, but the evidence has been suppressed by a conspiracy of the defenders of that other item of food, which I will refer to tonight as "the high-priced confection." It has taken diligent research for me to uncover the facts, but the results will justify my labors in the vineyard—or rather, the potato patch—for truth, though it appears to be swallowed in oblivion, will yet rise.

As anyone who has read Frederick Jackson Turner knows, the seeds of American democratic institutions were planted on the frontier. And as any student of American history knows, the frontier was a place where the simplest and crudest instruments of life had to do double duty. In cookery, the uncomplicated frying pan was the pioneer's first resource; the axe, rifle, and skillet were the weapons in the conquest of the wilderness. And what kind of dish do we make in a frying pan? I assure you, it is *not* the high-priced confection. That demands an oven—a more complicated piece of engineering—to say nothing of such exotic, un-American, and civilized ingredients as prunes or poppy seeds.

No, the simple cornmeal griddle cake—a kind of *ur*-latke—came first to the hardy sons of the wilderness, but with the coming of the Jews in 1654, and the utilization of the potato—originally native to the Americas, introduced into Europe by the Spaniards, transmitted to the English, and then replanted in the New World—with this juxtaposition of what was indigenous to our soil and a borrowing of European patterns, the latke sprang into being, as an authentically American and libertarian dish.

May I point out, in passing, that while I confine myself to literary expressions this evening, the very form of the two dishes suggests their relative identification with the principles of freedom and confinement. The latke is originally in the form of batter. Poured into the receptive, passionately heated *shmaltz*, it spreads freely into its natural circular form. The essence of the high-priced confection is that jam or filling is placed within the rigid limits of a shell of dough. Let the judicious draw their own conclusions as to what kind of personality will eat *that* kind of food and meanwhile hypocritically pretend to affirm democratic faith.

By the time of national independence, the close identification of the American mission and the latke had already flowed into our literature, and it has been expressed throughout the history of that literature in poems which, regrettably, the authors saw fit to suppress from their published works for fear of retribution by the determined anti-latke and pro-aristocracy Establishment. Diligent work on my own part amid hidden manuscripts, however, has produced some interesting examples of these buried works.

For example, an early national literary figure was the poet Joel Barlow. Barlow was a Yale graduate, and we cannot doubt that he learned of the latke there. Ezra Stiles, a former president of Yale, had been a great friend of the rabbi of the Newport, Rhode Island, synagogue; from this fount of Jewish learning he had gotten the secret of the latke, and passed it on to generations of sons of Eli. Barlow, among the most illustrious of these, is known for his poem on *The Rising Glory of America*, celebrating the achievement and future alike of the new nation, and also for his *Hasty Pudding*, a poetic paean to cornmeal mush. But who knows his manuscript poem, the *Latkiad*? Nobody, that's who! Here, however, is a passage which I have copied from it, in which the poet, in superb pentameters, makes allusions to the allegorical significance of the latke for the young republic:

> Within the pan, emitting hissing sounds
> The latkes lie, in perfect, golden rounds
> Was such a wholesome unity e'er found
> As that among th'ingredients here bound?
> This junction, at the blissful dinner hour
> Of egg, potato, fat and pinch of flour?
> Yea! One such union we may 'round us see
> The Union of these States, in Liberty!
> Then bless the latke, symbol of our great,
> Our peaceful, free and hungry Federal state!

I pass over an intervening period of development—egged on, so to speak, by the clock (a number-studded latke, the guardian of our hours), to the transcendental and romantic phase of our national letters. Most of you are aware that the poets of this generation, from Bryant to Emerson, were concerned with a variety of thematic materials, but among their central lessons were these. First, that man should seek in Nature the beauty and freedom and morality which he had within his own bosom as a child of Nature, but which was smothered by institutions. And second, that he should simplify his life as much as possible to bring out in himself those transcendent qualities which would make him a truly free creature, in harmony with the universe at large. Does it come as any surprise to you that Ralph Waldo Emerson and Henry Thoreau were *both* fond of latkes, and that Emerson wrote the following verses, which he read aloud at a latke supper held at Brook Farm?:

The Food Which Is the All

> When one has fled the thronging world,
>   To Nature's solitude
> He craves an earthly nutriment
>   A simple, soulful food.

> The lowly root, potato called,

Such aliment contains.
Consumed, it makes the psyche dance
To wild, bucolic strains.

The flower lies within the bud,
Divinity in all:
Likewise, the latke in the spud
Obeys the cosmic call.

Potato, stripped of skin, then ground
And purified by fire
Forsakes its gross, material form
For one sublimely higher.

And so the soul shall cast aside
Its skin of creeds outworn
And like the latke, in a new
Perfection be reborn!

Another phase of romanticism in literature was, of course, the glorification of our past and the search for meaningful legends that could be the substance of poetry. You are all aware of how Henry Wadsworth Longfellow dealt with Indian legends of the Lake Superior region. But are you aware that during his studies, he learned of the important role of the latke in Indian culture? Or that a section about how Hiawatha brought the latke to mankind was suppressed by the Board of Overseers at Harvard University, where Longfellow taught, because it was thought to contain too warm an endorsement of the Unitarian principle (embodied in the single latke as opposed to its three-cornered adversary of the prune filling). Harvard was Unitarian, but it did have public relations to think of even then. At any rate, here is the suppressed portion:

This is how he made the latke
Hiawatha made the latke
As great Manitou commanded
Manitou, who made great Latkes
In the sky by day, a Latke

Midst the stars by night, a Latke
For the warming of his children

Red and white, his hungry children
First he made himself the batter
Set aside a pan and platter
Round it was, and flat the platter
But the latke must be flatter

So he fried it on the downside
Till the downside was the brownside
Then he turned the downside upside
And the upside was the fried side
Round it was, without a third side
Or a narrow and a wide side

Thus like Manitou, Creator,
Made the latkes Hiawatha
Made of red men latke lovers
Led them lightly to the latke
And they named him ever after
Hia-latke, good-life-bringer.

Urged on by time's winged chariot—rolling swiftly along its twin
latkes—I pass to the local color school of American literature, of the
post–Civil War era, consisting of writers who tried to render an account of life in the simple and earthy patois of the common folk.
Among the best known of these bards of the barnyard was James
Whitcomb Riley, a Hoosier poet who was much beloved for his evo-
cations of the simple, rustic past of his Indian boyhood, wrapped
in an innocence like the early nation's. A manuscript discovered in
his family home shows conclusively that the latke formed an affec-
tionately remembered part of his childhood diet. Notice the contrast
between its simple goodness and the overcivilized urbanity of other
kinds of food:

When the frost is on the 'tater
And the latke's on the dish

Say, there ain't a thing kin touch it
Made from beast or fowl or fish.

Or some sour cream from Ole Bossy
Mooin' in the yard outside,
Glad to know she's bein' useful
To the home folks, bless her hide!

Yes, when life is kinder dreary
An' my spirits need a boost
I jes' long to be a youngster
Eatin' latkes like I uset.

Last of all, I wish to present to your attention a poem which dates,
I think, from the poetic renaissance that took place in Chicago just
before World War I. I found it tucked away behind a row of cookbooks in one of those side street bookstores; a drop of what appears
to be chicken fat obscures the author's name. I cannot tell whether
it belongs to Vachel Lindsay's work or Carl Sandburg's or some unknown ragtime versemonger's. But notice several things: its
unashamed use of the rhythms of popular speech in the dawning
jazz age; its vibrant vulgarity; the freedom with which its meter
changes almost from line to line, all expressing the dynamic freedom of the new poetry that was hurled defiantly at the strongholds
of genteel culture, where the Brahmins sat over their high-priced
confections and lamented the downfall of the older order:

Oh, listen to the latke rag
You latke-chompin' clan!
Can't you hear 'em sizzle in the pan, pan, pan.
Yeah, man!!!

Hear 'em fryin', hot an' noisy
They're the stuff, from Maine to Joisey.
Bindlestiffs and gandy dancers
Spielers, punks, and take-a-chancers,
Con men, cowpokes, saints, and grifters
All like latkes, with their snifters.

Big-time bosses and their floozies
Like them too; say, ain't they doozies?

It's on that old American plan,
That you get to eat those latkes, man!
Send the waiter back—
Give a smack, gulp, smack!
Tell him more, more, more!
Through that kitchen door!
Gotta gulp 'em down
'Cause I'm leaving town!

Yes, I hear that choo-choo round the bend
And I'm ditchin' my moll; we've reached the end
　　　She can't fry 'em
　　　And I won't buy 'em.
Choo! Choo! Smack! Smack! Yeah!

To quote Abraham Lincoln at this point, "I am loathe to close." Yet I hope that I have suggested to some extent the richness—the fullness—the broad circumference—of the hidden literature in praise of latkes composed by American patriots and liberals. As I began with a late eighteenth- and early nineteenth-century poet, so let me close with a verse from a contemporary minnesinger of Barlow's of whom you may have heard, one Francis Scott Key. It was while dining on his favorite repast that he watched the rockets' red glare lighting the skies over Fort McHenry, and it is small wonder that he incorporated a souvenir of that experience in the poem which a nation was to adopt as its unforgettable and unsingable anthem. The day may yet come when the sinister forces of censorship permit us to recite aloud the long-forgotten—or rather buried alive— verse which *really* concludes *The Star-Spangled Banner*:

May the time soon arrive
When latkes we thrive
And each bite shall delight us in being alive
And each patriot's heart shall enlarge with his girth
In this haven of latkes and freedom on earth.

Restoring the Jewish Canon

ALLAN BLOOM

I have a very short time, so I can barely outline the great scholarly task which lies before us if we are to restore the true understanding of Judaism which can be learned only from the proper study of the latke and the hamantash, a study which is in disarray, nay desuetude, due to the fragmentation of the university, of which this very panel is unhappily itself a reminder.

I should begin by remarking on the evolution of the debate itself.

In the patriarchal times, thirty-five years ago, there were latke persons and there were hamantash persons (then, actually, there were still men and women, but those were the olden days, and the words are almost without equivalent in our language). There were fierce partisans of one or the other, but the twain never met. Loyalty was central; no weak ecumenicism was envisaged.

Today we are forced to represent both. Now, I do not insist that this is wrong, but it can easily be misinterpreted. It is surely right to insist that Judaism is one; but it is a unity of tensions, containing being and nothing, life and death, reason and revelation, tensions that cannot be overcome.

In Indianapolis where I was born, it was the desert; and a conspiracy of Reform rabbis, trying to overcome our anguished longings for the Promised Land, served us up Manischewitz instant manna. Manna, it is to be remembered, is the undifferentiated unity out of which latke and hamantash were created, as night was separated from day, woman made out of man, never again to be confounded. These Reform rabbis, I say, tried to persuade us that the original unity could be regained, that our desert was Eden and that the latke and the hamantash are American cooking of Mosaic persuasion or, as we would now say, orientation.

In this they were dupes of Hegel's philosophy, which was nothing other than a subterfuge to get Jews to eat sweet-and-sour pork and thereby complete their assimilation. Hegel had the insight to see the oppositeness of the latke and the hamantash, and that they were both parts of Judaism, and attempted to overcome Jewish intransigence by inventing historical dialectic. The latke is the thesis, the hamantash is the antithesis; so he cunningly insisted that there must be a synthesis, and we can all relax.

It was on this basis that he insisted, as did Marx, his Jewish follower, that the morality of the Bible and the morality of the Greeks could be synthesized, producing an experience like eating a potato-filled hamantash or a prune latke.

As you can see from the foregoing, I bring a fresh and superior perspective to this important theme, and I must explain why.

I belong to the political philosophy wing of the Committee on Social Thought, an institution intended to survey and command all the sciences in relation to their proper end, the knowledge of the divine order. But there has been a revolt of the masses—the separate disciplines have emancipated themselves and are like former slave masters, passing off partial truths as the whole truth.

Specialization is a symptom of impiety. I must with all severity clarify our existential condition in relation to the latke and hamantash. The disciplines represented here are themselves indicative of the problem; and the harsh things we must say about them do not stem from a spirit of rancor, but from my well-known and uncompromising love of the truth.

The mathematician. What does he tell us? That the most important study is numbers and figures; that they get to the essence of things. But this in effect means that he can tell us there are 37, but not 37 what, not 19 latkes and 18 hamantashen. One latke is the same as one hamantash so far as he is concerned. Some science of essences! Plato saw this danger to the true sciences of the latke and the hamantash and wrote *Theaetetus*, in an attempt to teach mathematicians that they must first learn the *idea* or *form* of the latkes and the hamantashen and count them separately. But mathematical imperialism knows no bounds, and now we are in a pretty fix.

Even worse is economics. What is bad is not that economists say that man *can* live on latkes or hamantashen alone, but that they are vulgar materialists, not understanding the unique Jewish blending of matter and spirit in them which defies economists' categories. They think that consumer preference should determine the value of these sacred objects, repeating Locke's error that labor is the source of value. They think that there are proper terms of comparison between latkes and, say, pizza. Survival, bodily need, is all they know—as though anyone who was interested in health would eat Jewish food.

Actually they agree with Feuerbach's dictum that *man ist was er isst*, man is what he eats (as in *ess, ess, mein kind*) while the truth is *man isst was er ist*, man eats what he is. The economists have put the market in the place of the delicatessen.

And finally, the psychologist. Psychologists tell us that our states of soul make the world, not the world our states of soul; that, in Plato's formula, latkes and hamantashen are good because we are Jewish, not that we are Jewish because they are good. You see the relativistic consequences of all that. If you think that economists attribute nasty motives to human beings, wait 'til you find out what psychologists believe.

In truth they all follow their false messiah, Freud, who was secretly in the pay of, yes, the Manischewitz people again, who out of economic motives wanted to spread the appeal of their products beyond the Jews and turned to the psychologist for help. So Freud, for popularity's sake, interpreted the latke, the male, Maccabean food, as in its circular form symbolic of the male goal—I need not elaborate on this lascivious suggestion; and the hamantash—the joyous token of Esther's success, the female triumph—he explained by means of its angularity, its pointiness.

Propriety forbids my going further.

This certainly sold latkes and hamantashen, but you see what confusion it causes.

You should know that when you dream of circular and pointed objects it really means you have a suppressed desire for latkes and hamantashen. Actually the latke is circular because the circle is the perfect figure. But again mathematical narrow-mindedness causes us to reproach the form of actual latkes because they are not perfect circles; thereby we misunderstand God's essence of which the latke is the symbol, an essence beyond all forms, overflowing in its power, diffuse and uncontainable.

The hamantash's three corners represent the triad: God, Torah, and the Jewish people (its inner contents, prune or poppy seed, offer the possibility of purgation or an opiate). Thus our two great foods offer in tangible form the two great alternatives in Jewish life: mystical union with God and obedience to the Law. This is a tension to which there is no resolution and with which we must live. Happily the objects still exist, but bad interpretation bids fair to desacralize them. Nothing less than a reform of the university with the explanation of the latke and the hamantash understood as the one thing most needful will save us and restore us to our antique greatness.

Practically, the first thing to be done is to remove this debate from the control of the Manischewitz heretics and their agents, the Business School, and return it to the philosopher-kings; for only when wisdom and latke-hamantash coincide will evils cease.

Consolations of the Latke

TED COHEN

When first invited to this symposium I nearly declined, for I was not aware of how superbly qualified I am to speak on the question. Appearances to the contrary, I do not have a particularly strong Jewish background. But when the high purpose of the colloquy was explained to me, I could see that this is no trivial empirical topic, but rather that it is the categorical inquiry in which *data* are certainly an annoyance and probably an embarrassment. Being without any facts is an obvious qualification for successful investigation. In short, this is paradigmatically a philosophical issue. Indeed it is an a priori, transcendental question. I will dispatch it in two passes: first, from the standpoint of transcendental doctrine of taste (known vulgarly as finding the proof in the pudding), and second, from the even more sublime aspect of abstract metaphysics (known popularly as what's what, if anything). No need to delay announcing the conclusion: better to have it clearly in view from the start, for in philosophy it is often unclear from the argument itself what its conclusion is.

True philosophy leads to the latke. I shall not be showing that the latke is, in a simple sense, "better" than the hamantash. That cannot be done, for the latke and the hamantash are not commensurate. The hamantash is a very, very good thing of its kind. The latke, however, is a perfect thing. Now that I've laid the conclusion out, perhaps its transparent correctness is already evident to you. But perhaps not: it takes some practice and a little *chutzpah* to get these things straight; and so I will help you through the dialectical critique which leads to the celebration of the latke.

1. *Doctrine of Aesthetical Taste:*
The Latke as Pure Nosh

A perfect object of taste, a thing than which there can be no tastier, must appeal directly. Appreciation is not perfect if in order to enjoy an object fully you must take into account of what kind of thing it is. (This profound truth was first glimpsed in the eighteenth century by Solomon Maimon, who published a sketchy account under the pseudonym "Immanuel Kant.") That is how it is with hamantashen.

What is a hamantash? A cake. Not just any cake is a hamantash. It must be made of a certain kind of dough, it must have a specific shape, and it has to be folded around one of a few specified fillings; and it and its name are associated with a long, rich tradition. Of course we all know these things, but the point is that the essential experience of a hamantash—wonderful though it is—is predicated upon this prior conception. Most modern art is like this: you must know in advance what the artist thought he was doing if you are to make sense of his art. The realization that the hamantash is a form of aestheticized, proto-post-modernist art was first achieved by the dean of American philosophers of art, Monroe Beardsley, who made the point in the classic 1954 paper: "The hamantashen of the artist are neither available nor desirable as a standard for judging the success of the cakes" (written with Wimsatt, and widely reprinted: *The Hamantashenal Fallacy*).

As Beardsley saw, rigorous criticism forbids reference to these hamantashen-in-prospect. Thus it is a strict logical point that the delight in a good hamantash is not a matter of pure taste.

Not so with the latke. We all know latkes. Do not let a false empiricism persuade you that we had to learn this. It is innate in all rational *fressers* (gluttons): the form of the latke is indeed the form of oral intuition. The pleasure in a latke is the condition of all pleasures of taste. Think of it: a latke need have no particular shape, no required color, no conceptual preconditions (potato is best, of course, but even this is not of essence). The latke is the emblem of taste and art itself. And so: there can be no taste where there is not taste for latkes (*Tractatus Logico-Philosophicus*, the end).

II. Metaphysics of Being: The Latke as Substance

Here we are concerned with the proposition that not only do latkes exist, but that they must exist, that there could not *not* be latkes. Our problem here is not with the proof. The proposition is astoundingly easy to prove. The proposition, however, is impossible to say. There is no way to formulate precisely in words the necessary existence of latkes. We are grappling with an Idea of Reason, which has no adequate verbal expression. Wittgenstein once faced this problem and turned away, saying, "Wovon man nicht sprechen kann, daruber, muss man schweigen." (*Tractatus Logico-Philosophicus*, the end.) Or, in strict literal rendering, "If there's nothing to say, sit down and have a *knish*."

We, however, must be bolder. Let us take a number of imperfect formulations as ways of getting the inexpressible proposition across by analogy and suggestion.

Latkes necessarily exist. (Classical metaphysics.)

Whatever there are, some of them are latkes. (Free metaphysics.)

In every possible world there is a latke, though perhaps not the same latke. (Modal semantics.)

Necessarily, there is an x such that x is the square root of 2, and there is another x which is a latke. (Technical modal mathematical logic.)

When you see that these are but four ways of saying the same thing you will see what unsayable proposition I am saying. Now that we have the proposition—it is necessarily true that there are latkes—we can go for a proof. With necessary truths it is customary to say that they are self-evident and let it go at that, and that would be enough here for formal correctness; but we can go a bit farther. These proofs are not likely to be more perspicuous than the self-evident proposition itself, for those with metaphysical vision, but they may help others.

Why must there be a latke? Because the latke is an absolutely and perfectly simple thing, as is revealed in the fact that the idea of a latke is a clear and distinct conception of the mind. When we have such an idea (which is rare) we know that the thing of which the idea is an idea, must exist. If there were no latkes, the idea of a latke would not be so simple.

You are reminded, no doubt, of so-called ontological arguments, especially those meant to prove the existence of a supreme being. You are right: such an argument can be given for the existence of latkes, and I will return to this logos presently. First let us consider the treatment of this necessary truth in philosophical semantical ontology: the theory of possible worlds.

In every possible world, there is a latke. How do we know this? By discovering that it is impossible to imagine a world in which there is no latke. Try it.

First, imagine a world. Put in everything you need for a world; this is to be a whole world, not a fragment.

Now add in a latke.

Now take that latke out. It cannot be done, can it?

Some slower wits may suppose that you have imagined out the latke, but this is merely a misapprehension. When you took out the latke, where did you put it? Everything must go somewhere. Wherever you put it, it's still in the world: you didn't get it out of the world, you just shuffled it around. Thus every possible world has a latke. (You will notice that metaphysics is not so hard, once you get the hang of it.)

For a final proof of this metaphysical proposition, that there must be latkes, let us inspect a more classical mode of argument. Some of the most beautifully simple metaphysical proofs have been devised by the great Christian philosophers as ontological arguments for the existence of a supreme being. It is probable that you are most familiar with the arguments given by Saint Anselm. One of them is easily adapted to prove the necessary existence of the perfection of edibility.

This argument goes fast, and so you must be on your toes. The insight needed to follow the proof is simply the fact that just because something can be said it doesn't follow that the sayer can mean and think it. Sometimes we mistakenly suppose that something is possible because we can *say* that it is possible. But as the exemplary contemporary philosopher Dean and Professor Stanley Bates has said, "You can *say* anything; but not everything you say makes any sense. For instance, you can say 'It's possible that a prime number has many divisors,' but you couldn't really think that."

It was Anselm's genius to concentrate on the question of whether one can say—and mean—that there is no supreme being. It is an obvious adaptation to ask whether it can be supposed that there is no latke. Consider, "The *schlemiel* has said in his heart: 'There are no latkes.'"

The *schlemiel* can *say* this, but he cannot think it, for it makes no sense. What sense is there in a nonexistent latke? How can the perfectly edible be absolutely inedible? That makes no sense.

A world without hamantashen would be a wretched world. A world without hamantashen might be unbearable. But a world without latkes is unthinkable.

Q.E.D.

The Hamantash in Shakespeare

LAWRENCE SHERMAN

Who was William Shakespeare?

This question has defied the best scholarly minds for three and one-half centuries. Some critics have said his poems and plays were really written by the seventeenth Earl of Loxford. Others say that the true author was Francis (you'll pardon the expression) Bacon. Nonsense! Shakespeare alone, or somebody else with that name, is the true author. That this man of lowly origins—a humble hamantash baker by trade—could have written immortal verse comes as a surprise to some. But not to me. For a careful search of his sonnets and plays clearly reveals the man and the powerful source of his creativity.

The first clue to the mystery is to be found in Shakespeare's central play, *The Merchant of Venice*. In act 5, the young hero Lorenzo says to the beautiful Jessica: "How sweet the moonlight sleeps upon this bank! Here we will sit and let the sounds of music creep into our ears."

Here is a statement that appears to be poetic, clear, and straightforward. But how can it be both poetic on the one hand and clear and straightforward on the other? Modern literary criticism and centuries of Shakespearean scholarship teach us this is impossible. So we must look more closely.

The lines I've quoted are from the first folio. But we have the discovery of an earlier folio of Shakespeare's plays, the manuscript unknowingly used as the parchment wrapping of *kishke* in a Piccadilly delicatessen. It was found—the wrapping, not the *kishke*—discarded on a London dock. Thus, in honor of its place of discovery, it is now called the port-folio.

This new insight to Shakespeare reveals that Lorenzo's line, as originally written, was: "How light the sweet moon sits upon this bank! Here we will sleep and let the sounds of music ear in our creeps."

This is more satisfactory, I'm sure you'll agree. Yes, it's true that many think there's little sense to the revised lines. But that's because they read and listen with the eyes and ears of a person. It must be done with the eyes and ears of a PhD.

Consider again: "How light the sweet moon sits upon this bank!" But what is a bank? A place for deposits and withdrawals. As you know, food in Elizabethan times was so bad that most of what was deposited was quickly withdrawn. Hence, "bank" as used here clearly is a euphemism for the stomach. The line should therefore read: "How light the sweet moon sits upon my stomach."

But this makes little sense—unless you know that "moon" is a corruption of the Middle English word *mohn*. Lorenzo is paying tribute to the sweet taste of *mohn*, principal ingredient of the hamantash. Therefore, the first line actually says: "How light the sweet *mohn* sits upon my stomach."

Mohn, of course, is made from poppy seeds. And eating of the poppy leads to a state of euphoria and blissful sleep. Thus, the second line becomes clearer: when Shakespeare, through Lorenzo, says, "Here we will sleep and let the sounds of music ear in our creeps" he is, plainly speaking, telling of the effects of eating hamantashen, particularly the *mohn* in the middle.

I admit the passage is not crystal clear: "ear in our creeps" sounds a little strange to our coarsened poetic senses. But "creeps" is nothing more than a term derived from the Middle Yiddish (sixteenth century) word *greps*, a word still understood in scholarly circles. And "ear in" means to blend or to harmonize with. So the phrase "ear in our creeps" must mean "to harmonize with a *greps*."

Therefore, the two lines of poetry now are clear. Shakespeare is saying, through Lorenzo: "How light the sweet *mohn* sits upon my stomach. Here will I sleep and let my snores harmonize with an occasional *greps*."

But where does Jessica come in, you ask? A good question. The solution is simple, so transparent that it has been missed for 350 years. Jessica is the one who baked the hamantashen for the picnic. *The*

Merchant of Venice, stripped of its nonessentials, is really a Purim play—and a very good one when you consider that Haman, Morde-cai, and Esther never make an appearance. And Shakespeare's im-mortal hymn of praise to the hamantash—"How light the sweet *mohn* sits on my stomach"—refutes for all time any claim the latke may have to preeminence in English literature.

The hamantash hypothesis is clearly the key to Shakespeare's cre-ation of *The Merchant of Venice*. (One might even say—if he dares—that it is the key that opens the shy-lock.) Moreover, this hypothe-sis clarifies the underlying mystery of *Romeo and Juliet*.

Why were they a pair of star-crossed lovers? Why were their two households, both alike in dignity, feuding? The very names of the families give us the answer: Juliet was a Capulatke, Romeo a Hamantashague. Enmity, hostility, even hatred are the natural con-sequences.

Early in the play Romeo is mildly infatuated with another girl, Rosaline, of whom Mercutio says, "That same pale hard-headed wench, that Rosaline, torments him so that he will sure run mad." Notice the key words: "pale" and "hard-hearted." We know that Mercutio is, like Romeo, a member of the Hamantashague family. "Pale" must mean unripe, or underdone; and "hard-hearted" is the perfect description of a cold latke. Mercutio is calling Rosaline an underdone, cold latke. Romeo's infatuation, he is saying, cannot last—unless he is mad—for he knows that

Women who are cold, cold latkes
Cannot warm a young man's *gatkes*.

So when Romeo sees Juliet he loves her immediately, and soon says, "By yonder blessed *mohn* I vow."

She softly answers: "O swear not by the *mohn*, the inconstant *mohn* . . . lest thy love prove likewise variable." She does not know how to bake hamantashen and is trying to warn him away from his fatal obsession. The stage for tragedy is set. Truly, there "never was a story of more woe that this of Juliet and her Romeo."

We begin to see a pattern in Shakespeare's plays. When we note that the Dark Lady was the inspiration of his sonnets, the final clue to the secret of Shakespeare's power emerges.

"Dark" is the perfect word for the filling in a hamantash: it is black and it is hidden within baked dough. *Mohn* is made of poppy seeds (masculine, of course, or else it would be made from mommy seeds), but the other hamantash filling, prunes, is feminine; only women eat them, usually old women with irregularity. Thus the Dark Lady has two meanings—an absolute prerequisite in all literary criticism. The Dark Lady stands for Shakespeare's two favorite dishes—hamantashen and his constipated old mother. These were the twin sources of his inspiration.

For a few remaining skeptics, there is the sonnet of Shakespeare's, newly discovered, stamped on the skin of a kosher salami. It is Shakespeare's final testament, his *Lost Sonnet:*

Shall I compare these to a hot latke?
Thou art less fattening, more digestible,
While heartburn is the latke-eater's lot
(A fatal fact quite incontestable).

Consumed by that which he was nourished by,
The glutton soon cries out in vain, "Surcease,"
And then his appetite and he both die
As martyrs to an overdose of grease.

But thy eternal summer shall not fade,
Immortal poppy seed, O Hamantash:
The gourmet's appetite thou ne'er dost jade
When happily he has thee for a nosh.
Thy taste a taste of heaven must foretell.
While slippery latkes line the road to hell.

Jane Austen's *Love and Latkes*

STUART TAVE

This problem troubles me. I can't say that I ever thought much about it before, at least at the level of metacriticism. When asked to search out the sources of preference, the problem troubles me because, like most professors of the humanities, I suffer from the occupational disability of finding much to say on both sides, qualifying every assertion, balancing judiciously, gathering credit for avoiding a position, and for speaking in interminable sentences. This time I find it impossible to sustain that delicate equilibrium, and I think the reason is that this really is a humanistic decision and it goes to the center of my professional instincts.

I have, in the abstract, no disrespect for the hamantash, and I have over the years eaten one on the proper occasions, combining duty with pleasure, but even as I say this it reveals the moral as well as the aesthetic problem. It leaves me uneasy.

The eating of the hamantash is, in every sense, too sweet. You've eaten one, you've eaten them all. The very shape of the thing is antihumanistic, mathematical, limited, bounded. It achieves an easy ideal in the imagination combined with a ready satisfaction of taste, which is reductive and sentimental. There have got to be higher and more complex joys in God's world.

Now a latke is different, more liberating to a scholar of the humanities. It has a free form, not definable by any geometrical preconception or even description. Like the flakes from heaven, or the leaves of the trees, no two latkes are exactly alike. They are in that sense, without end. Who would ever eat *one* latke and think he had performed an intelligent or fulfilling act? You eat them to the extent of your capacity. Whatever space God has given you, you occupy. It is a holy thought. It is a complicated synthesis of divine contraries—latkes are real, even greasy, and they are infinite. One stops eating them not because the spirit is ever satisfied, but because one might burst and pass over into a higher form of existence, latkes forever, a state toward which the mortal soul can only yearn and is not yet ready to enter upon. The remarkable thing about all this union of opposites, and its validation, is that there is no guilt in stuffing yourself with latkes—think of that! No guilt!—a unique experience in a specific culture. It is a pure pleasure, and the only accusation of inadequate performance a man need fear is finishing too soon.

Now that last point, of cultural specificity is, I think, not a small one. The form, and the correspondent function, of the latke are distinctly different from the hamantash, and this difference has a widely resonant significance. Matthew Arnold recognized that, when he said that the hamantash was Hellenic, while the latke, Hebraic. He did not, however, understand fully the consequences of this insight, and in his preference for Hellenism he absurdly missed the point by rejecting the latkes because they were not sweet and light. I really think my grandmother was quite right when she would say, whenever the subject came up, "Matthew Arnold—what does he know from latkes?"

That imaginative freedom of form in the latke was better understood, as one would expect, by someone like Shakespeare, when he said, "The lover, the lunatic, and the latke are of imagination all compact."

Those lines require more explanation because of what may seem to be the curious inclusion of the lunatic, but in fact this extends the relevance of the text in a most revealing way. I have alluded to the cultural specificity of my subject, because it is sometimes only too easy to forget that latkes are concrete, but one must remember too that they can expand universally. Shakespeare, always mindful of these larger references, as well as the lesser subtleties, reminds us of this extended context by the inclusion of the lunatic, which we must here understand in its original, etymological reference to the moon and lunar matters, symbols of more universal concern.

I don't want to press this too far, but one should not dismiss lightly the importance of these alliterative linkages, since they have always been one sign of the ways in which the latke lends itself readily to poetic expression. Could you put "hamantash" in a poem? Only in grotesque parody, whereas we know how magnificently Swinburne succeeded in his *Lyric of the Latke*, in which, characteristically, he drives both the alliteration and the love to an extreme of shocking sensuality, as in that memorable line, "Lavish me with latkes, lingering lasciviously, labial, lingual, laryngeal; leave me not languishing for the lumpy lamellate latke I lust. . . ."

And so on, for a total of twenty-six lines. He even finds, brilliantly, a rhyme for "latke," which I forget at the moment.

But I want to conclude by citing an example of more classic sobriety, from a great author, an example that ties together several of the points I have been making on the interconnections of the alliteration and the love, the specific and the universal, and the guiltless indulgence, and to do this in an area where I do have a particular scholarly knowledge from my own research.

There is a unpublished and little known piece by Jane Austen, which I finally tracked down a few years ago at her home, in the back of a secret cabinet where she hid her most precious treasures, in a room strangely neglected by previous searchers.

Actually, it was in the kitchen. It is a sequel to *Sense and Sensibility* and *Pride and Prejudice* entitled, *Love and Latkes*, in which the sprightly young heroine comes to discover that love lies heavy at her heart, and the rather less witty hero finds out that latkes don't sit so light in the stomach either.

The turning point of the action, so to speak, comes as the heroine is mixing a batch. While preparing the potatoes, she skins her knuckles on the grater. Leah—for that is her name—nearly falls lifeless to the floor, but Louis—for that is his—fearful that she will not finish with the cooking, catches her up and bears her to the sofa, to their mutual embarrassment but better understanding. This advance to happiness is delayed, in the succeeding chapter, when he begins to eat the latkes, eagerly and rapidly, in such immoderate quantities that, in Jane Austen's proper words, he allows imperfectly articulated and indigested sounds of satisfaction to rise from his waistcoat and escape his lips. Leah is astonished at what, in her young and foolish prejudice, she perceives as grossness. "Had you behaved more like a gentleman, Sir," she cries, "you would have apologized for this shocking indelicacy. Are not you sorry?" But Louis replies, as well as he can with his mouth full, "Latkes is never having to say you're sorry." And she knows she loves him. There was perfect happiness in their union, because he loved her too, for the intelligence, the beauty, and the tested virtue he had found in her. As he delighted to explain in after years, "Could she make latkes!"

The Latke's Role in the Renaissance

HANNA HOLBORN GRAY

When Dear Abby was asked the question "Why do Jews always answer a question with a question?" she replied, "How should they answer?" And when I am asked do I give precedence to the latke or
the hamantash? I must reply, despite being absolutely sure of the answer, "How should the university answer?" This is not because I believe that the *état c'est moi,* whatever you may think. In fact, as president of the University of Chicago, it is my duty never to think.

Let me remind this audience of the stated policy of the university
as formulated in the Kalven Committee Report on the University's
Role in Political and Social Action, published and endorsed by the
Council of the University Senate in 1967: "[There is] a heavy pre-
sumption against the university taking collective action or expressing opinions on the political and social issues of the day, or modi-
fying its corporate activities to foster social or political values, however compelling and appealing they may be." Given my fidelity to the
idea of the university and the obligation it imposes for a colorless
neutrality, therefore, let me say in the most courageously forthright
and outspoken terms that both the latke and the hamantash are simply wonderful. We welcome them to our diverse, pluralistic, and tol-
erant community of scholars, as we have for a hundred years and
as we will for the century to come.

Fortunately, there is another path, that of the tenured professor.
I am accustomed to people asking me, with that peculiar kind of
careful courtesy usually reserved for those who have been recently
bereaved or incarcerated: "What did you used to be?" It is widely believed in scholarly circles that university administrators are failed
academics who have long since passed to the other side. For some-

one like myself, a Renaissance historian, any knowledge of Machiavelli is thought to be the fruit not of learning, or reading, but of the sordid instincts and sorry practices to which administrators bent on survival are prone. So I thank Professor Cohen for his grudging acknowledgment of my quasi identity as a historian and for this opportunity of presenting to you my scholarly and definitive solutions (1) to the problem of the Renaissance (i.e., the *Geistesgeschichtliche Problemstellung des Renaissance Forschungs und Periodisierungsbegriff*) and (2) to the understanding of the much misunderstood and maligned Machiavelli.

"God cannot alter the past," said Samuel Butler, "that is why he is obliged to connive at the existence of historians." This insight has been further developed by distinguished Jewish intellectuals. Thus Erwin Panofsky, asked to explain how he managed his elegant interpretations of iconography, in which everything fell so wonderfully into place, replied, "I bend the nail until I hit it on the head." That concludes my methodological discussion. And finally Hannah Arendt has given us a motto ideally suited to frame this Latke-Hamantash Debate: "I have yet to see any problem, however complicated, which, when you looked at it in the right way, did not become more complicated." This is certainly true of the relation of latkes and hamantashen to the Italian Renaissance.

Even this debate, as you can easily see by reading Pico della Mirandola's *Oration on the Dignity of Man*, is itself a product of the Italian Renaissance. Pico hit a nail right on the head when he wrote, "There are, indeed, those who do not approve of this whole method of disputation and of this institution of publicly debating on learning, maintaining that it tends rather to the parade of talent and the display of erudition than to the increase of learning." However, I myself propose to disprove these critics. I am about to increase your learning, and to do so with a becoming modesty, if also with conclusive erudition. So let us begin.

All discussion of the Renaissance must, of course, depart from Burckhardt's *Civilization of the Renaissance in Italy* and his assertion that the Renaissance, as a distinct period in human cultural and spiritual history, represented the discovery of the world and of man. Perhaps you think that is all there is to it; that I will tell you that the world is a latke, rounded and flat; man is the hamantash, the microcosm, the triangle enfolding as prune or poppy seed that spirit of individualism in which Burckhardt saw the birth of modern consciousness. You might think so, and you would be wrong. When I want your opinion, as the great Jewish thinker Sam Goldwyn remarked, "I'll give it to you." This is known as the Socratic method. It, too, has been used successfully at this university for a hundred years, as it will be in the century to come.

No, the problem of the Renaissance is indeed more complicated. It requires that we return with our hammers to that other old chestnut, the Renaissance as the revival of antiquity. We will now examine, as no one has yet done, the role and the tension of latke and hamantash in that revival.

The humanists of the Renaissance believed passionately in the value and objective truth of the ancient texts. Unfortunately, many of their texts were corrupted because of mistakes and mistranscriptions made by scribes (including Christian monks who were often shocked by what they thought they were reading—words like *nudum* and still stronger stuff—and who, as ascetics, were sadly hostile to food references). In addition, there was the problem of the absence of the letter *k* in Latin and of *h* in Italian, so that the latke in the one, and the hamantash when translated in the other, came out in rather curious and mysterious ways. Nonetheless, to the trained scholar familiar with the work of Renaissance humanism, they are recognizable. For the humanist of the Renaissance, if something existed in antiquity, it was good; if it existed in the greatest time of antiquity (i.e., before the Silver Age), it was really good; if it was in Cicero, it was canonical. The humanists adopted the ancient forms of the dialogue and debate. They could find the latke and the hamantash, and the debate over their relative merits, in ancient texts, could discuss the nuances and contrasts in many ways, and could relate these to ancient philosophy, poetry, and history. As divisions arose in Renaissance thought they turned out to be those of the latke and the hamantash, as we will see in the cases of Machiavelli and Pico della Mirandola.

In short, Renaissance humanism grew out of the revival of the latke, so prominent, though needing to be rediscovered, in the Golden Age of Rome, even before the decline of virtue and strength in her citizens. And what of the hamantash? It, too was rediscovered, in the Hamatus, which means "furnished with a hook," or "hooked." Some of the humanists were indeed hooked on the hamantash, especially those who read Lucius Appuleius and who found the Hamus, denoting a kind of pastry, in his *Metamorphoses*. But the literature associated with the hamantash in antiquity is far less rich than that of the latke, and its texts are primarily of Silver Age origin. Indeed, the *Metamorphoses* of Appuleius are better known by the title of *The Golden Ass*, which is assuredly not aristocratic or especially nice. Most humanists voted with their stomachs, not their seats, and with their classical tastes for the latke and would have nothing to do with the Golden Ass, as you should not, prunes or no prunes. Only someone like Pico della Mirandola, who was pretty much an adolescent and a syncretist to boot, became a hamantash addict. He liked to mush dissimilar things around together. The hamantash fit his taste for emblems and his puerile notions of magic and mysticism and the unity of knowledge and the poppy or mommy seed in the midst of the carapace within which the boring nub of universal truth might be found and consumed. This is known as Renaissance Neoplatonism, and you would be well-advised to give it short shrift.

But the tradition of the latke and its role in the unfolding of the Renaissance is of a different order. Here let me turn to Machiavelli and to the important revelation that emerges out of reading his work by the light of the classical latke scholarship that he inherited from his Quattrocento predecessors.

To Machiavelli, the relevant word was *latta*. That was perhaps because he spoke with a very heavy Italian accent—not surprising, perhaps, in view of the fact that he was Italian and wrote in Italian, too, and also because he liked to spend all day fooling around in a country café during his exile to Settignano, where all they had was Chianti and latke. The rustics there taught Machiavelli to call it that; the word means a tin plate or a thin plate or a slap or the crushing of a person's hat when you slap him on top of it. So it is quite relevant to the latke, and you can see it in not only the object, but also the way in which Machiavelli and his companions sat around and ate latkes and slapped each others' hats before calling for more. Machiavelli was not genteel.

In coming to the discussion of Machiavelli, I should emphasize that although he was a latke man, he has to be analyzed like a hamantash. This, among other things, makes him quite unusual. An example of such an analysis, although incomplete and basically inadequate, may be found in the work of the University of Chicago's own Leo Strauss, learned also in Jewish philosophy, entitled, *Thoughts on Machiavelli*. Strauss really went to town in pointing out that Machiavelli may never mean what he says; that the external surface hides a different meaning within, that he is master of deception, citing the letter to Guicciardini in which Machiavelli writes, "For some time I never say what I believe and I never believe what I say; and if it sometimes occurs to me that I say the truth, I conceal it among so many lies that it is hard to find out."

Strauss must also be credited with opening up a splendid line of investigation in his theory of silence, which states, roughly, that it is all very well to read the words on the page but what you should really be looking for is what the author does not say. That is where the true meaning is to be found: "The silence of a wise man is always meaningful." Here, indeed, we have the key which Machiavelli scholars have ignored.

There are a lot of things about which Machiavelli is silent. Let us examine the internal evidence. He never mentions his mother. He never talks about cooking. He is silent about Hanukkah. The old deceiver, so fond of posing extreme alternatives and then coming down resoundingly on the unexpected side, never poses the antithesis of latke and hamantash. What does all this add up to? You've guessed it. Machiavelli was Jewish—his silence makes that crystal clear. Not only was he Jewish, he was like all wise people, for the latke.

I suppose you probably feel, as I do, that I have said enough to show that the Renaissance problem is no problem at all and that Machiavelli is perfectly comprehensible once you understand the that his conception of *virtù* in history and politics is grounded in the revival of the Roman latke, flat, juicy, and oval like the Roman Republic he so admired.

It is fitting to contribute these conclusions to the world of scholarship at the time of our university's centennial, its celebration of learning, and its renewed commitment to complicating the uncomplicated, as it has done for a hundred years and will do relentlessly in the century to come, pursuing and disseminating the truth and the joy of discovery wherever they may be found.

The Approach through Bibliography

LEON CARNOVSKY

From *Alice in Wonderland*:

You are old, Father Jacob, the young man said,
And your beard has become very white;
    But I'd like to know why
    There's a gleam in your eye
When a beautiful lady's in sight.

When I was much younger, old Jacob replied,
My wife fed me latkes and cream;
    This built my virility
    Postponed my senility,
Now my eyeballs are right on the beam.

You are seventy-five, the young man explained,
But your youth, you seem to renew it;
    You can sprint, run, and dart
    Without straining the heart—
Pray, why can't the rest of us do it?

The reason is simple, the old man explained,
And your weakness can soon be rescinded;
    But you nibble and nosh
    On ye olde hamantash,
No wonder you all are short-winded!

You're an ancient of days, continued the youth,
And your mind ought to lose all its vigor;
      But you play jumping jacks
      Around Finer and Tax*—
What makes you so fast on the trigger?

The riddle is solved, you lump of a boy,
The answer is found in my diet;
      Three times every day
      I eat latkes au lait—
Now why don't the rest of you try it?

*Chicago colleagues Herbert Finer and Sol Tax

L'éternel retour (Eternal Return): The Dichotomy of Latke-Hamantash in Old and New French

My task is twofold. I must, first of all, add a touch of gentility to the proceedings at hand. By this I mean, of course, to insist on the traditional values instilled in every philologist and literary critic of the Medieval period, that is to say, scholarly caution, to the point of indecisiveness; gathering of supporting materials, to the point of suffocation. All this interlaced with prophetic generalizations, to the point of dizziness. Secondly, and more importantly, I came here not to praise the colloquium but to fulfill its highest aspirations, that is to say, to demonstrate the scholarship in action.

The latke-hamantash dichotomy is a symbolic expression of the oldest and most profound dichotomy in our civilization: The opposition of epic and Romanesque modes of expression. Latke is epic and hamantash is Romance. Let us look at the evidence. Latkes are made of uniform, homogenized matter. Most important, the content of the latke dictates its shape. Is this not epic, or even archiepic? As the latke mass spreads over the hot greasy territory of the pan assuming its proper shape, so does the epic matter assume its length according to the basic ingredients of the *materia epica*. There is no surprise, no foreign matter in the latke. There is a deep foreknowledge free from Romanesque suspense both in latkes and in the epic modes of narration. You know what you are going to find in the latke and in the epic, but is this true in respect to hamantashen and the Romanesque narrations of the French Middle Ages?

The one answer possible to this profound question is "no." In the hamantash the most important element is the surprise. Sometimes poppy seeds; sometimes, cherries; sometimes, heaven forbid, prunes. One does not know what to expect. Now, is it not true that sudden shifts in one's expectation—a constant, delaying, and frustrating of the pleasant shock of expectation—is a basic device of romance? And, if you are still doubtful about this symbolic parallelism between latke-hamantash and epic-Romance, let us return to the problem of shape, or more professionally, let us reevaluate the formal dimensions of the problem. Hamantashen are contrived; their shape defines their content. Folded into triangular preexisting, preconceived molds made not of metal, but of servile ideas, are not the hamantashen really like the Romance? Again, the answer is both simple and obvious: they certainly are.

Last, but certainly not least, is the problem of the homogeneity of taste. Like epics, latkes are uniform. In every bit, in every bite, the part represents the whole. But if we consider the hamantashen and the Romances, we realize that this is not the case. One bite is sweet, the other tart, the third neutral, and the fourth, mixed. Is this not the supreme proof that the latkes are epics and the hamantashen are Romanesque? It certainly is. And it is precisely this opposition which is inherent in the latke-hamantash juxtaposition which alone explains the success of our colloquium.

The examination of this archidichotomy in the French domain brings me to the final, clinching point. Why French, you might have asked? Well, there are many answers, but the best, as usual, is the philological one. The latke, you must know is as French as it is epic: it is an old Judeo-Greco-French term. The etymology of this beautiful term need no longer be shrouded in the mist of times and of ignorance. The original form of latke was of course *la tkne*. The word was usually pronounced by speakers whose mouths were full of latkes. This is the so-called L.F.S., i.e., *latkefressershproch*. The L.F.S. has caused the loss of *n*; this is easy to see, but what is the origin of this *latk(n)e*? The answer, I am proud to say, is simple. *Latke*, comes from *la tke*. *La* is of course the French definite article, as every undergraduate can see. *Tke*, with its *n* eaten away, is really the Greek *tekhne*, meaning "art," or more properly, "epic art"—which perfectly proves our demonstration. *Latke* is an epic and *tekhne* is epic art. If you worry about the loss of tonic *e* in *tekhne*, please don't. You should know how the Hebrew orthography treats vowels, especially important vowels. The loss of tonic *e* in *la tek(hn)e* is due to the simple but powerful orthographic influence of Hebrew.

I am sure that the archidichotomic aspects of the latke-hamantash pair, confirmed, proven and illustrated by the Greco-Franco-Hebrew origin of the very term *latke* demonstrate again the importance of this colloquium.

The Apotheosis of the Latke:
A Philosophical Analysis

ALAN GEWIRTH

I am very pleased to have been invited to participate in this famous latke-hamantash symposium. As I understand it, there is only one greater honor that can come to any professor—namely, winning the Nobel Prize. Since, however, the Nobel Prize is not awarded specifically for philosophy as such, but only under the much vaguer and more general rubric of literature, it is clear that in participating in this symposium I have reached the absolute climax, the supreme pinnacle of my professional career, and I have prepared my lecture accordingly.

In view of all this, some may be surprised to learn that when Rabbi Leifer first invited me to participate in this symposium, I said, "No," "non," "nein," and "nyet." I thought that if anything is obviously a nonissue, it is the question of the relative merits of latkes and hamantashen. It is indeed true that my beloved mother, being an immigrant from Bialystok, brought me up on lots of latkes rather than hamantashen. But still, I thought that this fact was of somewhat less than cosmic significance, and that there was nothing really to debate here.

I was about to turn the invitation down, when Rabbi Leifer lent me a tape of one of the past symposia. As I listened to the tape, I saw clearly for the first time two important facts that I had not seen at all before. The first that the question of the relative merits of latkes and hamantashen, far from being a nonissue, is in fact a philosophical issue of the deepest cosmic significance. The second fact, however, was that all the past debates have exhibited a kind of inconclusiveness that is also characteristic of most philosophical disputes.

Every year now, for nearly four decades, the greatest minds at the University of Chicago, and therefore, by definition, in the whole world, have applied their awesome intellects to this issue. But, despite this unparalleled concentration of immense intellectual erudition and colossal *chutzpah*, to the present day the issue remains unresolved. Each side remains entirely convinced that it is right, and each side remains utterly unconvinced by the other side. As a famous Yiddish proverb puts it, *Du bist nisht ah chochem*, which, translated very freely, means, "Who's on first?"

After a lengthy period of intense philosophical concentration, I have invented for this purpose an almost completely new methodology, which I have called philosophical or dialectical semantics. This methodology consists in showing how the very language that we use, and indeed that we must use, in discussing the latke-hamantash issue embodies subtle etymological features that point conclusively to the central place of the latke in all human thought.

Let me give you two clear examples of how this methodology works. First, consider the word I just used: "dialectical." It has long been recognized that most, even if not all, philosophical arguments proceed dialectically, in the sense of examining the statements made by persons who discuss the issues in questions. But what has not been recognized is the subtle philosophical etymology of the word "dialectical" itself. My research, using the arcane tools of philosophical semantics, has revealed that this word in its original form was "dialatkical." In other words, the very word for the central method of philosophical reasoning embodies the name of that majestic latke, which therefore figures universally in all philosophy.

Let me now give a second, even more conclusive example. Consider the very word, "philosophy." My researches have revealed the original pronunciation of this word was "philatkophy." In other words, the latke signified the very wisdom which all philosophers, by definition, are committed to seeking. From now on, therefore, I must insist on being regarded as a professor of philatkophy, and my colleagues, whether they like it or not, must acknowledge that, as members of the department of philatkophy, they are committed by their essential natures to recognize how their very calling reflects the grandeur of the latke. The word "philatkophy" means etymologically, of course, the love and pursuit of the latke, and it is this emotion, and indeed passion, that has animated all the great philatkophers.

I shall now demonstrate this thesis of the centrality of the latke by giving a brief survey of the main, but previously hidden, high points in the whole history of Western philatkophy.

Let us begin with Plato. It is not generally known that Plato's immortal writings, nowadays called "dialogues," were originally called "dialatkes." They were so called, of course, because they provided such a well-rounded, succulent intellectual feast. It was Plato's writings of dialatkes that gave his whole philatkophy its rich and yeasty flavor, both spiritual and earthy.

It is even less well known that Plato's greatest pupil, nowadays called Aristotle, was originally named "Aristlatke," from the Greek word *aristos*, meaning "best," and "latke." In other words, Aristlatke was so called because he was the best of all latke-eaters who participated in Plato's dialatkes.

There are many other evidences of the cosmic significance of the latke in modern philatkophy which the subtle instrument of philolatkical semantics discloses. Many of my insightful predecessors in this illustrious series of symposia have pointed out that the original name of the famous founder of British empiricism was John Latke. It has not been generally recognized that the noble latke also enters into the very core of Marxism. This is shown not only by the fact that the basic theory of Marxism is called dialatkical materialism, but also by the further fact the Karl Marx himself proclaimed that there would be no real justice in the world, that the exploitation of man by man would never cease, until there was a successful revolution by the prolatkariat. He called them the pro-latkariat, of course, because they were the class that advocated the eating of latkes as the supreme manifestation of human harmony and emancipation, and hence as the universal cure for constipation.

The latke occupies the very core of the moral and intellectual values of humanity, as my detailed arguments have conclusively demonstrated. My position has also been endorsed by all the great German philatkophers of the nineteenth century, from Begel to Knietzsche.

In conclusion, I wish to summarize the whole of my complicated but decisive argument, in two famous Yiddish proverbs. The first is this: *Abe du hust latkes, vos mehr darfst du?* I.e., "If you have latkes, what more do you need?" The other, even more famous, proverb, is this one: *Latke, schmatke, sei nisht ah nudnik!* Which, freely translated, means, "If you're through with your argument about latkes, then stop talking already!" So this is exactly what I shall now do.

Noshes

I shall prove categorically, once and for all, that latkes are superior to hamantashen. Second, I shall prove that latkes exist necessarily, i.e., in all possible worlds. Finally with what time remains, I'll discuss God.

My first argument for the superiority of the latke is quite simple. Even the greatest of hamantashen lovers will agree, I presume, that their delicacy is not as desirable as eternal happiness. Indeed, they should concede that *nothing* is better than eternal happiness. But this is sufficient, for surely a latke is better than nothing.

Now I can imagine some of you balking at the third premise in the argument. Notice however that the argument goes through even if the premise is denied. If it is not the case that a latke is better than nothing, then nothing is as good or better than a latke. In particular a hamantash is not. DAVID MALAMENT, *The Logic of Latke*

✡   ✡   ✡

Let us move to another masterpiece of the Judeo-American literary tradition, Herman Melville's *Moby Dick*. We need not follow the lead of certain Talmudic literary critics who read the title as *Moishe Dick*. Suffice it to note that be he Moby or Moishe, he is but a Johnnycome-lately to the venerable Yiddish trinity: Milche Dick, Fleishe Dick, and Pesach Dick. In the famous chapter 43, entitled "The Whiteness of the Whale," Melville confronts us with the fundamental and profound duality of the monstrous creature. Is the whiteness a symbol of virtue and goodness, or is it the emblem of terror and evil? Is the whale a three-dimensional latke, wallowing in its gargantuan and blubbery circularity, bodying forth the benign and virtuous aspect of nature? Or is the whale a gigantic hamantash, tapering from its massive triangular head to its tail fins, and incarnating the darkness, the malevolence, the evil in the universe? Ahab takes the whale for a hamantash, and carries his ship and crew with him to destruction. MARVIN MIRSKY, *Notes toward a Reinterpretation of American Literature*

✡   ✡   ✡

A little known fact involved the role of the hamantash in the sartorial history of the Thirteen Colonies. For what, if not the hamantash, inspired the design of the three-cornered hat, that great symbol of the great American Revolution? STEVEN WATTER, *Hamantash v. Latke: Which Is Superior?*

✡   ✡   ✡

Why is a university like a hamantashen baker?
Because they both knead a lot of dough.
HAROLD WECHSLER, *Latkes and the Art of Hamantashen Digestion*

Round Two

POTatoes, Rockin' Latkes, and Other Essence-ial Soul Food

The Latke vs. the Hamantash in an Age of (M)oral Crisis

HERBERT C. KELMAN

I am pleased to participate in tonight's panel, since it gives me the opportunity to present for the first time, for public consumption, the fruits of my many years of research on the internalization of moral values. It has, of course, been suspected for a long time that the moral posture of a man, of a group, of a nation, of a generation, is largely determined by what he ingests—by what he takes into his system, through whatever means. Until now, however, the exact processes whereby these effects take place have not been understood, not even adequately described. The reason for this failure has been—and I say this in all modesty—that, until I decided to address myself to this problem, there simply was no one who was able to bring to it the necessary combination of scientific acumen, historical insight, philological expertise, and theophilosophical sophistication.

My research is not yet entirely complete. As you will see from the data I shall present to you, the puzzle has almost been solved, but here and there a piece is still missing. Nevertheless, I decided to present my findings now because of the urgency of the moral crisis that we are facing today. I felt that I have no right to withhold information that can decidedly influence the future of mankind merely because of scruples rooted in a scientific perfectionism.

Let me begin, as scientists are wont to do, with some autobiographical comments, tracing the stops that led me to the discovery which, I am sure will in due course be rewarded with the Dow Chemical Prize for the use of scientific knowledge in the promotion of human welfare. These experiences, by the way, will be published in the near future in a best seller entitled *Triple Helix*, which you will immediately recognize as the molecular structure of the hamantash.

I sensed, whilst still in my early teens, that the conflict between the latke and the hamantash is more than a mere *Purimspiel* for casual entertainment. Underneath the lighthearted banter, I felt, there lay a deeply rooted antagonism reaching back into the long ago past. For years I took, half consciously, the side of the latke, eating its material manifestations in large numbers to the accompaniment of a concoction composed of baking soda and water. But I began to rebel, and my rebellion took the form of probing research into the origins and meaning of the latke-hamantash controversy. It is these circumstances that bring me before you today as the man best equipped to place this controversy in its proper bio-psycho-socio-historico-pharmacological perspective.

Bio-psycho-socio-historico-, you say, all right. But pharmacological? Yes, my friends. Some of you may think that the problems of drug use and abuse and their impact on the moral fiber of our youth are innovations of the 1960s. In fact, however, these are problems of long standing that my own research—as I shall soon show—traces back at least as far as the days of the Babylonian Talmud. Ever since then and throughout the centuries there has been a struggle between those who have sought to destroy the foundations of the moral order by giving themselves and seducing others to the use of narcotics and hallucinogens, and those who have sought to preserve basic principles of morality by consistently combating and counteracting the corrosive influence of these instruments of moral degradation. The struggle is, of course, particularly poignant today because we find ourselves in an age of moral crisis in which the very survival of Judeo-Buddhist values is at stake, but it is continuous with a struggle that has been raging for at least fifteen hundred years.

In this historical struggle, the latke and the hamantash have been the major symbols of the two antagonistic forces confronting each other across the moral abyss. The latke has been the symbol—and, I might add, the instrument—of the destructive use and abuse of dangerous drugs. The hamantash, on the other hand, has served as a symbol and rallying point of the struggle against this evil and of the rehabilitation of the addicted. Much of this has been largely unknown because the latke movement, like other conspiratorial movements, has carried out its activities secretly and relied on allusions and dissimulations for the propagation of its vicious cause. The hamantash movement, in response, has had to fall back on similar devices. In the old Messianic tradition, the standard bearers of the hamantash have had to hurl themselves into the *klipe*—into the heart of sin—in order to wrest from it the holy sparks held captive there and thus lead man to his liberation. Thus, the struggle between the two sides has proceeded through allusion and indirection, accessible only to those initiated in the kabbalistic tradition. It is only because of my readiness to combine painstaking research into ancient sources with brilliant theoretical insights that I was able to encode the relevant documents and to uncover their mysteries.

The evidence for the central role of the latke in a drug cult that extended over several centuries is overwhelming. Let me just give you several illustrations.

Take, first of all, the basic ingredients of the latke as described in several old recipes. Universal, of course, is the use of the potato, the true meaning of which, I am sure, will be obvious to all of you once I call your attention to the first three letters of that so-called vegetable. Like all great discoveries, this is self-evident once it has been pointed out, but it takes genius to first grasp the connection.

Less self-evident is the meaning of onion juice, an ingredient listed in many of the recipes. This is a slightly disguised reference to *opion*, the Greek word for poppy juice, from which, of course, many narcotics are derived. It is not entirely clear from the documentary evidence whether latkes actually contained these ingredients, or whether they were merely used as appetizers and legitimizers at drug parties. The indications are that, at least on many occasions, they actually did contain chemical ingredients, and that they were available in a variety of flavors, such as hashish and paregoric.

Evidence that, on some occasions at least, latkes served as appetizers at parties at which drugs were ingested by other means comes from a little-known treatise published in Rome in 1420 under the title *Magnum Opus*, which is, of course, Latin for "a large amount of *opius*," *opius* being the past participle of "opium." On page 726 (and I translate from the original): "Twice a week, young men and women gathered privately to eat latkes, drink tea, and share sympathy." The reference to tea is obvious. Sharing of sympathy probably refers to the passing around of reefers, since *pathy* comes from the Greek word for "grief," which is an obvious homonym for "reef." In any event, the evidence clearly shows that latkes were associated with drug cult gatherings.

Two pieces of evidence come from the seventeenth century, from the movement that formed around Shabbatai Zevi, the false messiah. It is now quite clear that this movement was basically a drug cult, with hallucinogens like marijuana and LSD serving as sacraments in its secret rites, and that the flights of fantasy for which Shabbatai Zevi himself was known were basically drug-induced states. First, it is significant to note that Shabbatai Zevi's second wife—whom he later discarded for the infamous Sarah—was named Miriam Yochana, which is the Hebrew equivalent for Mary Jane. As was customary in these cults, Shabbatai Zevi bestowed upon her one of the basic sacraments, which explains the hitherto mysterious origins of the term "marijuana." Secondly, the documents of the Shabbatian movement abound with invitations to and descriptions of the Latke Supper Dances, which apparently were marked by wild orgies and wide-ranging hallucinations. I assure you that the initials of these Latke Supper Dances were not chosen at random but were meant to convey to the initiated the content of the agenda that lay before them. This also shows, by the way, that contrary to accepted accounts, it was not Dr. Albert Hoffman, the Swiss chemist, who first synthesized LSD in his laboratory in 1943, but Shabbatai Zevi around the middle of the seventeenth century.

For my final piece of evidence let me turn to the Chasidic movement. An exhaustive survey of the records shows that the early days of the movement were marked by an intense power struggle between proponents of the latke and those of the hamantash. The former, who were mostly graduates of Shabbatian drug sects, were actively trying to subvert and take over the Chasidic movement. They almost succeeded, particularly among the Cockneites of western Macedonia and southern Uzbekistan, who characteristically drop the initial aspirant and therefore pronounce Chasidic as "acidic." It was easy to persuade them, therefore, that "acidism" as they called it, was essentially a cult of acid-heads. Fortunately, this particular power struggle was won by the forces of moral righteousness. The final blow to the latke-eating infiltrators was dealt by the advent of

the Lubavitcher wing within the Chasidic movement. They succeeded where others had failed because they clearly focused their
energies around the hamantash as the central symbol in the struggle against evil. They named the three corners of the hamantash
chochma, *bina*, and *deat*—wisdom, understanding, and knowledge—
and this became the primary slogan of their movement.

This leads me to the second major component of my research effort—the investigation of the role and meaning of the hamantash
in the century-long struggle between the forces of degeneration and
the forces of moral rectitude. Let me start out by quoting to you the
first references to the hamantash in the published literature. The reference comes from the Babylonian Talmud, order *Feasts*, tractate
Bubbeh Mayse, folio 72b. I will first give you the quotation in the form
that has been commonly used, even though—as I shall point out
shortly—this is based on an interesting misreading of the original
text which had not been discovered until I came along. It reads as
follows, and I translate from the Aramaic, "And you shall form them
into three-cornered pockets and they shall contain the meat of the
pitted plum and the seed of the poppy plant." Seed of the poppy
plant, of course, refers to poppy seeds, which is the origin of hamantashen filled with poppy seeds or *mohn*. Meat of the pitted plum has
been interpreted as prune preserves, which explains the second traditional filling for hamantashen. Here, however, is where the textual
error was made. As you may know, in Aramaic—as in Hebrew—only
the consonants are used in the spelling of words, not the vowels. In
the original text, therefore, the following letters appeared:

PTTD PLM

This was read, by the rabbis, as pitted plum. From internal evidence, however, I was able to deduce that the intended meaning was
potted palm which, as you can see, has the same consonants, but of
course, different vowels. The intention of the Talmud was the baking of a pastry filled with the meat of the potted palm, in other
words, coconut, not the meat of the pitted plum. It is truly fantastic
that, because of earlier shortcomings in philological research, we
have been eating prune-filled hamantashen for fifteen centuries,
when we should have been eating coconut-filled ones. Fortunately

I was able to uncover this error, or we might have been eating prune-filled hamantashen for another fifteen centuries.

Now, keeping the correct text in mind, what does this Talmudic quotation allude to? "Meat of the potted palm" refers to marijuana: as the botanists among you will know, the coconut palm is very similar in appearance to the cannabis or hemp, from which marijuana is derived. Hence marijuana has, for many centuries, been referred to as potted palm—or pot, for short. "Seed of the poppy plant" alludes to opium, which is, of course, a derivative from poppy juice. Thus, when the Talmud speaks of hamantashen as containing the meat of the potted palm and the seed of the poppy plant, it refers to the two major types of dangerous drugs: the hallucinogens and the narcotics.

But note the used of the word "contain." Its most obvious meaning, of course, is to hold or include, as an ingredient in a recipe. But it can also mean to restrain, to hold back, as in containment of the atheistic Communist aggression. The Talmud, as is characteristic of much esoteric writing, is using a very clever play on words here to describe the basic symbolic function of the hamantash: that is, to contain—to hold back, to ward off, to counteract—the evil influence of the drug cults as symbolized by the latke. It is no coincidence that a three-cornered pocket was chosen as the central symbol, since three is a holy and magical number, widely used in the kabbalistic tradition as antidote to evil spirits. The three dimensions of wisdom, understanding, and knowledge, identified by the Lubavitcher Chasidim, intersect in the three corners of the hamantash, to become the three key weapons in the struggle against moral decay—a struggle which, by its inherent nature, must rely on political rather than military means.

But the hamantash was not merely a symbol in the battle for men's minds, used in efforts of propaganda and education against the insidious forces of the latke. It was also the major instrument in an active, many-faceted therapeutic program, designed to cure drug addiction and drug habituation. You are witness to a truly historic occasion, for this is the first time that I am publicly revealing this major discovery—the high point of my many years of research on this problem and a path-breaking contribution to medical history.

My first inkling that I was on to a discovery of unusual proportions came with the realization that "hamantashen," the plural of hamantash, is a precise and perfect anagram of Maneshthana —the Four Questions with which the traditional Passover seder starts out:

HAMANTASHEN

MANESHTHANA

In light of my research, I knew of course, that such an anagram is no mere coincidence and no doubt reflects a direct and significant historical connection. I proceeded, therefore, to delve into the sources and, step by step, I was able to discover the links. Very briefly, here is what I found.

In the Talmudic period, Purim was an occasion for mounting an extensive public health campaign, in which people habituated or addicted to drugs were encouraged to come to specially arranged briefing and educational sessions. These sessions, which were informal in nature, were designed to inform participants about the existence of a special therapeutic program and to encourage them to sign up for it. Hamantashen were served during these sessions, as the traditional refreshment, and the hamantash was, of course, also the symbol of this entire movement.

The actual therapeutic program was conducted a few weeks later, at Passover time. As a matter of fact, this is the origin of the Passover seder, which was really an elaborate, and I might add very effective, procedure for the treatment of addicts. Much of this had to be done secretly and with the use of allusions and code names, such as "hamantashen" and its anagram "maneshthana," because of the opposition of the latke-eaters, who were violent and ruthless in their mode of operation. Hence, of course, the historical identification of the seder with secret services; it stems from this era, rather than from the period of the Spanish Inquisition as is generally held.

The key to the therapeutic program used on these occasions is provided by the Maneshthana itself. The Four Questions allude very clearly to the four major components of the treatment program. The first question states that "on all other nights we may eat leavened or unleavened bread, but on this night, we may eat only unleavened bread." "Leavened bread" in Hebrew is *chametz*, from the same root as *chometz*, which is "vinegar" or "acid." Thus, the first question simply refers to the first part of the treatment: the total withdrawal of acid or whatever other drug that patient was addicted to. The second question states that "on all other nights we may eat all kinds of vegetables, but on this night only bitter herbs." This alludes to a chemical treatment, using a derivative from the bitter-tasting pulp of the *Kranus Judaicus*. The third question asks why "on all other nights we are not commanded to dip even once, but on this night twice." It, of course, refers to a form of hydrotherapy. Finally, the fourth question, which asks why "on this night we all recline," is an obvious reference to a form of psychoanalytic treatment. This last item not only indicates that psychoanalysis, in its fundamental aspects, predates Freud by at least fifteen hundred years, but it also suggests that these four-pronged therapeutic programs continued to be carried out in secret throughout the centuries, at least until the end of the nineteenth century, and perhaps even today, which may account for the apparent success of Synanon. As you may know, Freud did not discover psychoanalysis until his middle years. Earlier, he was very much interested in cocaine and was possibly addicted himself. I believe that I have found the historical link between these two phases of Freud's work, and also an explanation for the apparent parallelisms between his writings and the Kabbala. It would seem that he joined a Maneshthana group to cure himself of cocaine addiction, and that there he learned about the ancient form of psychoanalytic therapy which he then elaborated into the set of techniques that one now associates with his name. This, of course, is a whole other chapter in the history of medicine, which I shall leave for another occasion. For the moment, let me merely conclude by expressing my gratitude to the hamantash for having sustained man's moral needs throughout the centuries and my own oral needs throughout the decades.

Influences of Latkes, Hamantashen, and Jewish Cooking in General on the Roots of Rock 'n' Roll

WILLIAM MEADOW

I am going to talk about the influences of latkes, hamantashen, and Jewish cooking in general on the origins of rock 'n' roll music. But first we must situate the discussion in a historical context. Jewish cooking has had important influences on music, long before rock 'n' roll. After all, the most widely recognized baroque piece ever written was originally entitled, *The Challeh-luyah Chorus*. More recently, in the American classical mode there was Aaron Copland's *Bialy the Kid Suite*. And, perhaps the greatest Jewish cooking opera of all time was Modest Mussorgsky's masterpiece, *Borsht Godunov*.

Indeed, there is a little known story about how that opera was named that leads us into tonight's discussion of latkes and hamantashen. You may not realize this, but Modest Mussorgsky was heavily influenced, not by his great Russian contemporary Rachmaninoff, but by that other major cultural Rach—Rachy and Bullwinkle. Yes, it's true, Modest Mussorgsky was a Rocky and Bullwinkle cartoon addict. Naturally, he gravitated to the two Russian characters, Boris and Natasha. In one episode, Boris and Natasha had made some exploding latkes to use against Rocky, Bullwinkle, and their colleagues. Late in this episode, we find Boris scrubbing the latke pan to try to remove all the traces of the sinister efforts, in the event that Rocky or Bullwinkle should return and find evidence of Jewish cooking by these unlikely types. Boris is scrubbing, scrubbing, but it's hard to remove all those traces of burnt-on potato and onions. Finally, he turns to Natasha and says, "Darling, do I have to keep scrubbing this latke pan?" She turns to him, inspects the pan carefully, and finally says, "No, no, Boris, Godunov!" And that is the first, but not the last, evidence of the dominance of latkes over hamantashen in the growth of music in the twentieth century.

Let's move now to rock 'n' roll. The name "rock 'n' roll" was coined by Alan Freed, a Jewish DJ from Cleveland. He took the name from "latke roll," a snack given him by his mother when he went to listen to the "new music," for which up until that time there had been no name. When, in the fifties, there was talk about this new sound being a short-lived fad (unlike say, eating goldfish, or stuffing college students into Volkswagens), Danny and the Juniors emphatically sang, "Latke rolls are here to stay; it will never die." They followed that hit up with "You've got me rockin', got me rollin', got me boppin', got me strollin' at the lat-ke … It's the taste sensation that's sweepin' the nation, eat a lat-ke."

How about Shirley and Lee? They sang, "Come on, baby, latke good times roll." Here's a *Jeopardy* question: He was one of the most dominant figures in early rock 'n' roll. He married a thirteen-year-old girl; he ritually set fire to his piano at the end of his Saturday evening performances (clearly an elaboration of the havdalah service at the end of Shabbat). His greatest hit was, "Whole Latke Shakin' Goin' On." Right: "Who was Jerry Lee Lewis?" And who *was* Jerry Lee Lewis???? It can be revealed here tonight that Jerry Lee Lewis was the son of the Jewish baking matriarch, Sara Lee Lewis.

Finally, what many consider the founding group of r 'n' r reflects the obvious influence of Jewish cooking in its very name. They weren't Bill Haley and the Comets, as people have come to know them. No, their original name was—Bill Haley and the Chometz. And did they sing about hamantashen, made of flour???? No, they did not. They sang of potatoes, and onions, and *shmaltz*: Their most famous song, "Rock around the Clock," was originally titled "Latke 'round the Clock."

Now, where were hamantashen in the fifties? Very weakly represented indeed. Probably the most important hamantash proponent was Eddie Fisher. Remember when he sang about his preference for hamantashen filling: "Oh, my poppy, to me you are so wonderful; Oh, my poppy, to me you are so grand." And then there was

Perry Como, who sat on a stool in a cardigan sweater and sang about more general food groups: "*Kashe* falling star and put it in your pocket." And Dean Martin had a great Pesach hit with "When the moon hits your eye like a big pizza pie, that's a *moror*!" But there are other hamantashen fillings besides the poppy, even in the fifties. Andy Williams had a huge hit with, "Prune River, wider than a mile," although what exactly constituted a mile-wide "prune river" in the context of overindulging in hamantashen filling is something we'll not get into here.

The Latke-Hamantash Debate in the late fifties was ultimately resolved along the traditional Marxist lines (though more Groucho that Karl). There was a thesis (latkes)/antithesis (hamantashen) that resolved into a synthesis. And what was that synthesis? It was clearly marked by the ascendance of the ultimate fifties Jewish food rocker. We don't even have to look more deeply here: Jewish influence in r 'n' r had by this time come out of the closet (or, more accurately, out of the pantry). His name was Buddy Challeh. His signature hit, "Maybe Baby," was a crossover version of the earlier, more ethnically Jewish, tribute to his grandmother, "Maybe Bubbeh." The appeal of Challeh went far beyond narrow religious borders. The Isley Brothers wrote a Pentecostal ecstatic paean of their approval for braided *challeh* when they came up with "Twist and Shout."

Remember Fats Domino? It can be revealed here tonight that to avoid anti-Semitic prejudice in the r 'n' r industry he had his name changed: it used to be Shmaltz Domino. He, of course, sang the original version of "Good Challeh, Miss Molie." And of course the ultimate Jewish cooking group of the early sixties were named simply the Challies. But their ethnic roots did not stop with their name. No, their greatest hit was the ultimate lament over one, well-formed matzah ball for another, less fortunate colleague. Remember? "He ain't heavy, he's my brother." I think probably the entirety of the influence of Jewish cooking on early rock 'n' roll (or latke roll, as we now know it) was captured by the Five Satins (originally a Jewish group from New York's garment district). They sang a song that captured the culinary stresses of keeping kosher in an increasingly secular world. The crossover version was known as "In the Still of the Night," but the original version went something like this:

In *gefilte* the night
When I held you, held you so tight
And I really kept the faith
Promised I'd never, never eat *traife*
In *gefilte* the night.

One of the most important conflicts for a Jewish boy was between his girlfriend and his mother. More specifically, his mother's cooking. Brian Highland sang a song about a Jewish boy leaving for summer camp, who would not miss his girlfriend's kisses, but rather his mother's food: the later cover of this song was called "Sealed with a Kiss," but the earlier version went something like this:

I don't want to say good-bye
For the summer
Knowing the food I'll miss
So let us pledge
To eat in September
And seal it with a *knish*.

The Beach Boys clearly not only took sides in the Latke-Hamantash Debate, but also weighed in with their opinion on another major Jewish division: "Latke go surfing now, everybody's learning how, come on a Sephardic with me." But where are the hamantashen? The Beach Boys sang, "Blame it all on the surfer's prune," which many authorities (and I count myself among them) have taken as another derogatory reference to the consequences of overindulging in filled hamantashen. Lou Christie was more broad-minded about hamantashen: "Two fillings have I." Then there is the Rolling Stones lament, "I can't get no hamantashen."

We must conclude with a rock 'n' roll song that dealt poignantly with one of the ultimate Jewish dilemmas—love outside the faith. It's a song sung by a young girl, who is torn by her love for a non-Jewish boy. Their relationship is foundering, and in her grief she looks for guidance from the great Jewish traditional teachings, the Torah, the Talmud, the Rabbis, Rabbi Akiva, Rabbi Hillel, and the Ba'al Shem Tov. One night, poring over the teachings of Rabbi Hillel, she finds teachings that resonate. We find her crying inconsolably on her

pillow over the author's words, weeping as she tries to reconcile rab-
binical teachings with lost love. The original version of "Tears on My
Pillow" went something like this:

Oooh, oooh, waaaaah, oooooooh, oooh,
You don't remember me
But I remember you—
'Twas not so long ago
I learned you're not a Jew.

Tears on my Hillel (shoo do bop),
Pain in my heart,
Over you . . . you. . . .

Love is not a gadget,
Love is not a toy.
When you find the one you love,
You hope he's not a goy.

If we could start anew
I wouldn't hesitate.
I'd gladly take you back
If you would congregate.

Tears on my Hillel,
Pain in my heart,
Over you . . . you. . . .

The Fundamental Jewish Cuisine

PAUL ROOT WOLPE

At Hanukkah or Purim in universities all over the country, academics are invited to take part in the annual Latke vs. Hamantash Debate. The purpose of the debate is to argue about which is the archetypical Jewish food, latkes or hamantashen. When invited to participate, I took my mandate very seriously. The job of the sociologist is, after all, to uncover the hidden, to make problematic the obvious, to explore the unexamined assumptions underlying social convention. Therefore, after pondering the question deeply for ten or fifteen minutes, I determined that a fundamental flaw has been made in the choices of cuisine offered. Any true historian of Jewish cuisine knows that neither the latke nor the hamantash is the true, primordial, undisputed champion of Jewish cuisine. No, there is a food more basic by far.

At first, foods like latkes, hamantash, or matzah come to mind. But why? We only eat these foods on particular holidays, once a year. How can they be basic? *Kreplakh*, *kishke*, and *knishes*? Too much cholesterol. *Cholent*, *tsimmis*, or *shmaltz*? Too fatty. A bagel with a *shmeer*? That is almost as good as it gets, but there is one better.

And that food is: herring.

Yes, herring. Jews, both Ashkenazic and Sephardic, are from the Mediterranean basin, and there is not a country that borders on that great sea—European, Asian, or African—that does not eat herring. In Northern Africa, Western Europe, and Eastern Europe it sustained us, and if the oneg Shabbat at my synagogue is any indication, it sustains us still.

I remember the first time I encountered herring. I was about five years old, sitting on my Zayde's knee. He was having his usual breakfast before *shul*: herring in cream sauce on leftover *challeh*, with a seltzer water chaser. He lovingly spread the herring on the *challeh*, making sure to get plenty of cream sauce and onion, and when he put it into his mouth, a little dribbled down his chin, which he wiped with his finger and licked clean. I'll never forget that moment: sitting there on Shabbat morning, secure in my Zayde's arms, watching him eat that herring, I thought to myself: "That's disgusting! The most revolting thing I ever saw. I'd sooner eat chopped liver!" Little did I understand at that point the central place of herring in Jewish history and culture.

Herring was prominently featured at a dramatic debate between Hillel and Shammai. In the greatest fish story of the Bible, Jonah is swallowed, as you will recall, not by a whale, but by a *dag gadol*, a big fish. Hillel insisted that the fish was a herring. Shammai, on the other hand, insisted that it was a sturgeon. Hillel made a passionate plea for the herring, noting, for example, that the lowly sardine is in the herring family, while from sturgeon we get that most expensive of foods, caviar, and since Jonah was a simple man of the people, G-d would not have sent a sturgeon to swallow him. Hillel almost had the rabbis won over, when Shammai produced a fisherman holding a typical, twelve-inch herring. "Could this have swallowed Jonah?" he asked incredulously. Then, in one of the most dramatic moments in the entire Talmud, Shammai flung open a curtain, behind which was a twenty-foot, two-thousand-pound sturgeon. "This could have swallowed Jonah!" he proclaimed. It seemed Hillel was sunk. However, never underestimate Hillel. He casually plucked a grape from a nearby fruit basket, and, holding it up for all to see, asked in a meek voice, "You see this grape? It is a tiny thing. A simple man could carry hundreds of grapes." His voice began to get louder. "Yet the Torah tells us that when Joshua sent spies into the land of Canaan, it took two of them to carry back a single cluster of grapes. How big were those grapes? The size of an olive? Hardly. The size of an *etrog*, perhaps? No, even more, even more." Now Hillel was shouting. "They were undoubtedly at least the size of Shammai's head! And if the Riboyne shel Oylem could make a grape the size of Shammai's head, he could make a herring the size of a sturgeon!" Rashi comments that, shaken by this defeat at the hands of the master, Shammai retired to Natanya and opened a shwarma stand.

The Torah itself often speaks of herring. Note this excerpt from *Song of Songs*, the famous passage known as the "Psalm of Psolomon the Pseaman":

I cast my net over the waters, and the catch is good.
Yea, my lover's lips are like twin herrings,
pan-fried and drizzled with lemon butter.
I will serve them on endive leaves;
I will garnish them with goat's cheese and sprigs of parsley.
Verily I will feast upon them,
first carefully removing the bones.

In his monumental, twenty-volume work, *Herring and the Jews*, a noted herring expert develops the idea that herring is a metaphor for Jewish existence, signifying the unity of the Jewish people. He tells the following tale about how the Ba'al Shem Tov first became famed in the Jewish community. A rival rabbi, the Ba'al Na'alyim Tovim, challenged Shem Tov to explain how Hashem could create Jews of so many different types. How could Hashem create Sephardim, he asked, who actually eat rice on Passover and talk funny, making no difference between the letters *saph* and *taph*? The great Chasidic master commented: "There is herring in cream sauce, and there is herring in wine sauce; still, the essence of each is herring. So, too, there are Sephardic Jews, and there are Ashkenazic Jews, yet the essence of each is their connection to the Torah. The rest is just sour cream and onions."

Herring's metaphorical properties go deeper than Chasidic anecdotes. Herring is *pareve*; it fits in with any meal, just as the Jews scattered around the world fit into many countries. All around the herring are the dangers of the deep—the shark, the barracuda, the jet ski. Still they survive. And, like the Jew, the herring understands the importance of keeping their children in schools.

Need I go on? Herring and the Jews, the Jews and herring—it is part of our souls, not the food of special occasions, not the latke of Hanukkah or the hamantash of Purim, but the Jewish manna, the food that has sustained us. Mel Brooks once commented: "We mock the thing we are to be." And now I find myself, every Shabbat morning, spreading my herring in cream sauce on *challeh*, and licking the dribblings from my fingers. My kids absolutely refuse to watch me eat it. And that is how it should be.

Noshes

The consumption of hamantashen represents nothing if not an act of faith. Faith in our people and the love of parents and G-d. As a child, I can vividly recall those occasions when, on Purim, a great plate filled with hamantashen would be passed around. The adults would "ooh" and "ah" as they chose their prune and _mohn_-filled cakes. But what were children to make of this? Prune was out of the question. But what of the mysterious _mohn_, this viscous, black-spotted jellied stuff? Children are about as likely to eat _mohn_ as they are the jellied mess in which gefilte fish is packaged. Yet, with the urging of parents, and our faith in their love—our parents would never ask us to do anything that might harm us in the least—we tried it. And, while _mohn_ is an acquired taste, preferred by adults 3 to 1, and while we wouldn't rave about it, we survived. So, _mohn_ and the hamantashen of which it is an integral part equal survival and faith. The two great traits of the Jewish people.

Can the same be said of latkes?

Don't be silly.

STEVEN WATTER, _Hamantash v. Latke: Which Is Superior?_

✡   ✡   ✡

For a latke lover, and a nutritional biologist, the stuff of the latke is its essence. The stuff is the potato and the oil in which it is fried. Indeed, it is the energy content of the oil with its nine calories per gram that has the strength and richness to convert the foundational potato at four calories per gram into the more highly charged latke that brings to mind the role of courage, strength, and faith of the Maccabees and their opposition to Hellenization. GODFREY S. GETZ, *Reflections of a Nutritional Biologist*

✡   ✡   ✡

A hamantash is nothing more than a prune pocket or, at best, a poppy-seed pocket. With that we have disposed of the hamantash. Thus, without loss of generality, the problem has been simplified to something with some starch to it: the latke.

I don't like quoting higher authority to prove a point, especially when a logical deduction has already done it so amply. But I claim that the State of Israel supports my thesis. How do I know? I'll give you a proof. What is the national anthem of Israel? "Hatikvah." Where does the tune of "Hatikvah" come from? Most people agree that it came from the tone poem, "The Moldau," by the Czech composer Smetana. Now *smetene* is the Yiddish word for sour cream. Has anyone here ever seen anybody eating a hamantash with sour cream? Q.E.D. ISRAEL N. HERSTEIN, *The Latke's Lament*

✡   ✡   ✡

The Babylonian Talmud records the famous dictum of the noted sage Rava (Megillah 7b): "A man is obligated to get drunk on Purim to the point where he can no longer distinguish between 'Cursed is Haman' and 'Blessed is Mordecai.'" Maybe that's why the holiday is called "Pour 'em." MURRAY H. LOEW, *New Imaging Methods for Discriminating Hamantashen from Latke-induced Gastric Distress*

Round Three

Accentuate the
Positivists

The Voyage on the Bagel:
In Honor of the Darwin Centennial

ELIHU KATZ AND JACOB J. FELDMAN

Sociologists, like psychoanalysts, historians, and others, have a peculiar approach to the physical sciences. We don't claim to understand their concepts or experiments—that would be foolhardy; instead, we are content simply to tell them where they get their ideas. It's nothing more, that is, than going up to someone and, as gently as possible, telling him that what he is saying may or may not be true but, after all, that that is hardly interesting anyway; what is *really* interesting, we say, are the social and psychological factors that led him inexorably to his idea. If the idea didn't occur to *him*, we conclude, it would have occurred to somebody else just like him. Call it one-upmanship if you must: in sociology, we call it the sociology of knowledge.

It is in the spirit of this branch of our science that we approach this year's symposium, which, if we were informed correctly, is an appendix to the Darwin Centennial, contributing approximately as much as that organ contributes to the functioning of the body. This year, as in the past, we continue steadfast in our determination to avoid taking sides. As sociologists—we have said before—we have no values, though our less scientific colleagues cannot seem to digest this and conspire again and again to force us to one side or the other. But we shall not yield. We present the facts as we see them and leave the policy-making to others.

From the peculiar vantage point of the sociology of knowledge, then, the obvious first question is: where did Darwin get his ideas? Specifically, how did the idea of the survival of the fittest happen to occur to him? The answer, it so happens, is really quite simple once you have a theoretical frame of reference. Indeed, ask yourself the question: what kind of worldview would *you* have if *you* took a "voyage on a bagel"?

Consider the attributes of such a vessel. The decks are slippery and curved. One must teeter back and forth between the unguarded abyss at the outer edge and the yawning cavity in the center. Consider spending years in such brinkmanship, skirting daily disaster, parading around and around in single file, afraid to come abreast of your neighbor for fear that you will lose you footing. Indeed, what more appropriate view of the world for a voyager on a bagel than the survival of the fittest? We are suggesting, in other words, that Darwin's view of the world was influenced by the structure of the life-space aboard his ship. The accompanying table illustrates how the shape of the ship conditioned the social relations of the voyagers and how the structure of these relations, in turn, gave rise to a particular worldview.

Thus far, of course, we have merely stated a hypothesis. But we can go further; indeed, we propose to test the hypothesis. There are

		SHIPBOARD LIFE-SPACE	SOCIAL RELATIONS	WORLDVIEW
BAGEL		+ Slippery + Curved + Danger at outer rim and inner rim	+ Individualistic single file + Hostile + Competitive	+ Survival of the fittest
LATKE		+ Flat + Danger at outer outer rim + Safe in the middle	+ Huddling together in the middle + Cooperative + Interdependent	+ Survival of the outcast + Mutual aid
HAMANTASH		+ Protective ship-body + Shletered interior + Safe all over	+ Welfare state	+ All species survive

TABLE 1: "The Voyage on the Bagel," by Katz and Feldman. Artistic collaboration: Farrand Ennis.

a number of ways in which one might go about this, but perhaps the most cogent approach would be more or less as follows: if life aboard a bagel gives rise to an ideology of the survival of the fittest, then life aboard other sorts of ships ought to give rise to other sorts of ideologies. Here, then, is a testable formulation of our position, and what's more, we are prepared to plunge ahead.

Let us consider, first of all, what kind of worldview would result from a voyage on a latke. First, let's see if we can find somebody who took a voyage on a latke. That's easy: think of *Kon-Tiki*, or better yet, Huckleberry Finn. Their vessels were completely latke-like. Except in a severe storm, or when evil human elements intervened, life aboard ship was relatively placid. The danger—be it noted—was only at the very edge; one could fall off, as Huck actually did when he was frightened one night. The chief social-organizational principle on a raft is the huddling together at the middle where it is safe, and from this architectonic fact, it follows—of course—that people aboard ship make friends and become closely interdependent. Indeed, it is to the interest of those aboard to prevent individualistic wanderings-off to the edge, a fact which is vividly illustrated by the well-known folk expression among navigators, "Don't rock the latke." Now, what kind of a worldview emerges from a voyage on a latke? Ask Huck and Jim, the two marginal members of society who helped each other to survive. Reflecting on their mutual aid and their interdependence, Huck says, "I'd see him [Jim, the runaway slave] standing my watch on top of his'n, 'stead of calling me, so I could go on sleeping; and see him how glad he was when I come back out of the fog; . . . and he would always call me honey and pet me and do everything he could think of for me, and how good he always was; and . . . the time I saved him by telling the men we had smallpox aboard, and he was so grateful." From a voyage on a latke, then, there results quite a different ideology than from a voyage on a bagel. Instead of the survival of the fittest, we find the survival of what many might consider the unfittest; and instead of lonely individualism we find mutual aid.

Finally, consider the hamantash. Compared with the bagel and the latke, the hamantash-shaped vessel is an inspired construction indeed. Life on this vessel goes on inside, where it is soft and warm and womb-like, shielded from all the elements. Who took a voyage on a hamantash? Why, Noah, of course—as any handy Golden Book will confirm. And what was Noah's view of the world? That's easy: all species—two of each kind—survive.

Here we rest our case. We have tried to establish—and table 1 repeats our story in summary form—that the ecology of one's life-space influences one's view of the world. In Darwin's case, five years on a bagel were responsible for a view of the world in which only the fittest survived. Voyaging on quite a different vessel, Huck Finn shows what happens when the unfit unite to survive. And, finally, Noah—with divine inspiration—shows that a voyage on a hamantash leads to a worldview in which all species survive.

Moral (for possible use of policy-makers): cast your hamantash upon the waters.

The Latke and the Hamantash
at the Fifty-Yard Line

MILTON FRIEDMAN

I must confess proudly at the onset that my research on our problem is as yet unfinished, so I must content myself with a mere progress report. I will present it chronologically. Then you will know how I tackled the problem and where I now am.

One of the great curses of what goes under that name of social science is the failure to separate sharply positive from normative science. If home economics is to be a positive science, we must first of all discipline ourselves sternly to repress all value judgments, all matters of personal preference, and to lean over backward to be objective and impersonal. This is a particularly hard task in the present instance. The question we are discussing has played so large a part in the early childhood life of all of us, has had so strong an emotional intent, that I fear none of us can use the words "latke" and "hamantash" with the proper degree of scientific detachment. Accordingly, as a just step in a scientific analysis, I propose to rename the objects of study. I toyed with the idea of referring to them simply as L & H but quickly realized that the computer would be happier with fuller designations to keep our dependent variables distant from the heart of independent, paranoid, and schizophrenic variables we shall have to introduce in a full analysis. Accordingly I propose to call them Lob (for lobster) and Ham (for hamantash).

Having renamed them, my next step was to feed all the basic data into the computer. I am sorry to report that all that came out was hash. Three graduate students are now writing doctoral theses on this unexpected result.

On further analysis, I realized that my error was the one which has become so common since the improvement of high-speed computers—feeding the data to the computer at too early a stage without a full mathematical analysis. Accordingly, I returned to first principles: what is the key scientific issue? To ask the question is to answer it. Obviously the basic question in the functional relation between the marginal rate of substitution of Lob for Ham is the indifference between the relevant consumer units and the parameters describing the psychological, gastronomical, and intellectual characteristics of those relevant consumer units.

This major advance having been achieved, I turned to the next step: Who are the relevant consumer units? How can we get a representative example? You will pardon my immodesty if I say that, thanks to my earlier work, this question hardly detained me at all. Numerous studies have demonstrated conclusively that I happen to have the rather unique property that my own personal characteristics furnish in a sample of one, a thoroughly representative sample of those higher psychological, gastronomical, and intellectual qualities that can alone determine relevance. I know you will wonder whether I am not smuggling in illicit value judgments when I refer to "hyper" qualities. Unfortunately time is too brief to enable me to deal fully with this subtle issue. I can only assure you that you need have no qualms on this score. Ever since that pathbreaking scientific pronouncement of Louis XIV, "L'état, c'est moi," it has been a recognized principle of scientific sociology that one man can be a microcosm of a complex society. And my conclusion that, on this issue, I am that man, has not been reached carelessly.

This issue settled, the next question is the mathematical form of the desired relation. Here, thanks to a remarkable instance of that serendipity of which Professor Merton of Columbia has made us all aware, I was able to make a major breakthrough. If we replace the lob by a lavine of an ellipsoid of revolution and replace ham by a regular tetrahedron, we can carry on our analysis in a Rumanian space of aleph dimensionality.

I fear that I shall not be able to show you the proof. I can only tell you that it is elegant, delicate, and concise. And the result is a formula rivaled only by the famous Einstein equation $E = MC^2$ for simplicity, fruitfulness, and profundity. The result is $L = q\text{H}2/3$, where q will, I am sure, hereafter be known as the Friedmanian context.

Hamantash, Bagel, or Latke:
Who Has the Power?

The question tonight, implicit in the title given this symposium, is the same question we debate day in and day out: who has the power? Can the latke and the hamantash help us to answer this question?

Three classical views of the distribution of power in society have been promulgated by eminent sociologists: society as hamantash, society as bagel, and society as latke. In presenting these views for your delectation, I will examine not only their ingredients, but also their origins. From the peculiar vantage point of the sociology of knowledge, I ask: how is it that these three views have emerged? What in the personal experience of the three thinkers who presented them led to their conceptions of power in society? Why is it that visions of hamantash, bagel, and latke danced through their heads? Why not sugarplums?

We begin, then, with the views of Reb Chaim, otherwise known as C. Wright Miltz. C., or Chaim, as he was fondly called by his non-Jewish friends, has argued persuasively that the distribution of power in America closely approximates a hamantash. At the pinnacle we have a power elite, a trinity of industry, military, and government united into one—a hamantash within a hamantash. Below, said Reb Chaim, is a dominated mass of powerless, atomized individuals. But why did he view the masses as isolated, alienated, atomized? Reb Chaim, we have uncovered, had a distinctive preference for the singular texture of poppy-seed hamantashen over prunes. Where would the bewailers of alienation be today, had he preferred sticky, clinging, integrated prunes?

How are we to account for Reb Chaim's conspiratorial view of the operation of the power structure, his idea that the power elite secretly manipulates the masses and makes all the decisions? Those who have studied the madness of hamantashen baking will quickly understand. Imagine, if you will, the child Reb Chaim bouncing on his mother's knee. What did he see? First, the swift hand of his mother dipping into the innocent mass of poppy seeds and dropping them into a corner of an open, unthreatening triangle of dough. And then, her deft fingers swooping down and quietly folding up the sides of the dough, trapping the unsuspecting poppy seeds within, knitting up the seams, and leaving them powerless, trapped in the darkness. Indeed, with such experiences, how could he have seen the powerful as anything other than manipulative?

Let us now move on to the view of society as bagel, the view of the renowned sociologist Reb David Riesman. Reb David has claimed, as you recall, that there is no power elite. Society consists of numerous veto groups, each protecting its own interests, but none dominating the whole. These veto groups, says Reb David Riesman, exercise power only on issues of special interest to them, never undertaking to centralize power and to develop effective leadership for the total society. The result, as Reb David discerns in his penetrating analysis of society as the bagel, is a power vacuum in the middle.

But this is no simple bagel. The vision indelibly imprinted on Reb David's mind as he daily watched the endless stream of bagels rolling through Zayde Riesman's factory, was that of bagels within bagels within bagels—a vision not unlike that of the prophet Ezekiel. Each smaller bagel has become a veto group, which, like the encompassing society, is afflicted with the same emptiness, the same lack of assurance, the same lack of inner-direction at the center.

What kind of world is a bagel? It is a world without straight lines, a world without corners, a world without sharp intersections and firm decision points. In such a world a man cannot gain a solid footing; he cannot attain a clear sense of direction. All revolves constantly without beginning or end. With his bagel conception of society, it is simple for us to understand why Reb Riesman has characterized modern man as other-directed. You and I, he says, careen about our bagel world, unable to set our sights on changeless goals, buffeted from crust to crust, always reaching out to others for guidance.

The final view of power I am constrained to digest with you tonight is that of society as latke. This is more a vision of the future than a description of the past. It is the view of participatory democracy. While it has been difficult to trace this dream to one man, my research indicated it originated with that renowned Democrat, Allard Lowenstein.

And what is this vision of participatory democracy? Of society as the latke? It is a vision of the day when there will be no more power elite, when power will be distributed evenly throughout society, with small lumps of cultural diversity spicing the bland homogeneity of WASP society like the coarsely grated potato and garlic in his Bubbe's latkes.

Reb Allard teaches us that this vision can be attained only through heated confrontation, through sizzling and bubbling in the frying pan of history, but it will prevail, if we are willing to rub our fingers to the bone against the harsh grating opposition of hamantash-oriented elitists and bagel-brained veto groups. Like the Maccabees of old, the youthful followers of Reb Allard *will* emerge victorious to realize their vision of latke society.

The Latke, the Hamantash,
the Common Market, and Creativity

JACOB GETZELS

That the hamantash is related to creativity was shown in one of Eliot's experiments, a follow-up of his earlier brilliant work in discovering the male-female dichotomy. He presented a random sample with a question to which each subject was required to give a random answer. The question was: "The word hamantash brings to mind . . ." Seventy-five percent of the subjects said, "poppy seed," 15 percent said, "lechvar," 10 percent said "mohn."

The results speak for themselves. The preference for poppy seed can mean only one thing: identification with the germinal, i.e., the creative, principle. Poppy is of course a variant of "pop," or father, the maker; and seed is, of course, seed. In this connection it is not irrelevant to note a common educational expression, "those seedy professors," clearly a relic of the days when professors were creative. *Lechvar* immediately gives rise to Lochinvar and the whole Don Juan complex, again the seminal principle. The word *mohn* is by no means as neutral as some claim. On the one hand, *mohn* evokes *le mond* or *mundus*, i.e., the world of all creation, and on the other, *mohn* is also of course *Mund*, the German word for "mouth," a psychoanalytic concept having obvious oral-creative connotations.

A small number of respondents were struck by what they called the "filled" or "pregnant" quality of the hamantash. Those respondents connected the word *mohn* with the English word "moon," which represented for them a feminine symbol. This is, of course, plain moonshine when one considers the far more common reference to the man in the moon than to the woman in the moon. Eliot could only account for these responses as representing some sort of neurotic distortion.

It is perhaps these same disaffected people who are now proposing the feminine or latke theory of creativity. In this theory, creative people see things as Gestalten, have a need for closure, and are always eager to finish up everything in sight—typical latke eaters. Unfortunately, if I may permit myself a value judgment here, education—and especially higher education—has been deeply influenced by the latke theory of creativity, so plausible on the surface, so profoundly false underneath. Indeed, deans and admissions officers seem to have swallowed the latke theory whole. Witness their unceasing search for the well-rounded student. They do not stop to think that these well-rounded students indulge in circular arguments in the classroom.

Noshes

Fresh from our successes in dealing with the problem of poverty, delivering the country from the scourges of mental illness, juvenile delinquency, crime, and racism, today's social worker stands ready to apply his special skills to present circumstances.

Let us look at the concept of social rolls. Roll theory is as old as the bagel itself. The lowliest peasant had his little *bulkele*, on up to the loftiest majesty, the kaiser. Each one knew his place, his roll, as it were. The theory of social rolls is clearly applicable here. Bagels, *bialys*, *bulkelach*, kaisers, *tzibbile bundehs* are social rolls. They are easily adaptable to social gatherings. One can stand around at a social gathering, easily munch a roll, and still move about engaged with other people. I would classify the hamantash in this category.

The latke, however, is a pain in the neck. It violates all the rules of the theory of social rolls. Stand around at a social gathering with a latke between your fingers, sour cream, applesauce, grease dripping on your hostess's white shag rug, and you will understand the real meaning of roll theory. STEPHEN Z. COHEN, *Latkes, Hamantashen, and Social Work*

✡   ✡   ✡

A colleague, a fellow sociologist, claims that immediately upon reading our study he had the feeling that we were wrong. Unable to confine himself to just feeling this, being the worst kind of positivistic empiricist, he rushed right out to prove us wrong. He administered another projective test based on the technique of chains of word association. I must express my shock at the crude sampling mistakes which he committed, thus entirely invalidating his study.

Our colleague found that people associated from the word "latke" in the following sequence:

> *Latke—applesauce*
> *Applesauce—gander ("what's sauce for the . . .")*
> *Gander—Newfoundland*
> *Newfoundland—Vikings*

which our colleague claims is an inner-directed association pattern since, he insists, the Vikings were obviously inner-directed. But *we* did not find that at all with our sample. We found this sequence:

> *Latke—potatoes*
> *Potatoes—Ireland*
> *Ireland—Mayor Briscoe*
> *Mayor Briscoe—the Diaspora is a good place for Jews.*

There can be little doubt, we think you'll agree, that Diaspora-orientation, for Jews, is virtually synonymous with other direction.

In the same way, we were able to discredit our colleague's findings with respect to the hamantash. While he found

> *Hamantash—poppies*
> *Poppies—veterans*
> *Veterans—conventions*

and thus other-direction, we found

> *Hamantash—three-cornered hat*
> *Three-cornered hat—de Falla*

De Falla—Valencia
Valencia—oranges
Oranges—Jaffa
Jaffa—Tel Aviv

which, being the opposite of Diaspora-orientation, indicates clearly that the hamantash is an inner-directed Zionist symbol. ELIHU KATZ, *Continuities in the Sociological Study of the Latke and the Hamantash*

✡   ✡   ✡

Because of its inferior status among the majority of people, Latke Lovers continually challenged the hamantashen faithful to debates. And the Latke Lovers used a particular style of debate: if the hamantashen supporters asserted something, the Latke Lovers would deny it. If the hamantashen faithful denied something, the Latke Lovers would assert it. It didn't matter what the content of these assertions were: the Latke Lovers set the pattern. These people were so tenacious that this style of rhetoric has become one of the cornerstones of the Social Sciences. NANCY L. STEIN, *The Judah Fables*

✡   ✡   ✡

As Von Neumann and Morgenstern point out in *The Theory of Games*, it is not enough to say there is a relation between the latke and the hamantash and football in most societies. This relationship has been well studied and the specific relations well documented. A latke is made on a griddle iron; football is played on a gridiron. The hamantash has three points; a goal in football gets not two points or four points but exactly three points. Clearly those relations are functional, not accidental. More basically, ask the question: where is football played? On a lot, of course—an obvious derivative of "latke." And indeed, in smaller states like Rhode Island where there isn't room enough for big football lots, they play the game on small lots, which are in fact called "latkes." JACOB GETZELS, *On the Relationship among Latkes, Hamantashen, and Football*

✡   ✡   ✡

People who are considering estate planning options are often thinking about ways to reduce their tax liability, and the comparative tax
implications of holding assets as latkes or as hamantashen are almost too obvious to require comment. Not only do the latke bearers benefit from the oil depletion allowance, but consider the value
system of the holiday to which the latke owes its origin. Hanukkah
is epitomized by the giving of Hanukkah *gelt* (money), the passing of
assets from parents and grandparents to children and grandchil-
dren. This is the paradigm of estate distribution that most clients
find most attractive. Contrast that with the paradigm inherent in the
Purim story, in which Haman pledges the transfer of Mordecai's assets into the royal treasury, exemplifying the flow of assets from individuals to the government, a recurring theme in the Book of Esther which celebrates the excesses of an elaborate bureaucracy and
ends with Mordecai's raising taxes.

It is neither the latke nor the hamantash that best represents the
estate planner. So I respectfully submit that our symbol should be
that which reflects our usual condition, that of quandary—and I
move that our symbol should be . . . the pickle. JOHN LASTER,
An Estate Planner's Perspective on Latkes and Hamantashen

Round Four

Luminous, Luscious Latkes: Bewitching, Beguiling Hamantashen

Ode to the Latke

EDWARD STANKIEWICZ

A Jew develops from the cradle
A craving for a *knish* and *knaydl*.
He'll glorify *gefilte* fish,
But I, I love the latke dish.

A Jew'll pursue with zest and mania
The whiff of a *kishke* from Rumania;
He'll call a Shabbos-meal his princess,
And lick his fingers after *blintzes*.

A Jew will put his soul and talent
Into a *cholent*, known also as *schalet*;
He'll bless the Lord or shout "hurrah"
When he tastes the garlic of *ptcha*.

Many a Jew has made his slogan
A pot of *kreplakh* or *pirogen*,
But I say, "*Kreplakh*, *shmeplakh*, nothing
Delights me as much as a latke puffing."

Some Jews will hail with *shofar*, bugle,
The glory of a *lokshen kugel*,
But I, I am in a blissful state
When I see a well-stacked latke plate.

And what is in a hamantash?
A hamantash is but a *nash*!

A latke sends you, it inspires,
And titillates with fresh desires.

Pity the gentile and the heathen,
What have they got that we don't have, *Yidn*?
Though some may insist with serious mien,
That the gentile, too, has a fine cuisine.

That the Turk has invented shish kebab,
Which no fine palate can afford to snub,
That Indian *kurkum*, or Chinese *foo-yung*
Is a feast from the East for the choosy tongue;

That the French with his endive salad and brie,
Has made European history,
That Italian spaghetti at one glance
Transports you into the Renaissance,

That even the German sauerkraut
Can't be thrown to a vulgar snout,
Not to speak of *gevetsh de Pešt*,
Which is praised by gourmets from Budapest.

Faced with the gentile's cuisine and variety,
A Jew will not lose his nerve or piety,
Recalling his mother's strudel dessert,
He will say, "I have those things *in dr'erd.*"

A Jew brought up on Mama's culture,
Will shout, "Throw those dishes to the vulture!
I will not touch that stuff at all,
If I can have a matzah ball."

No Jew could possibly endorse
That yell, "My kingdom for a horse."
But he would give his shirt and *gatkes*,
For a couple of Mama's latkes.

A Jew, he almost genuflects
When't comes to food; not even sex
Can send such shivers through his spine,
"Oh, *mechaiyeh*, mm, divine."

But in our garden one dish is most noble,
Ancient, regal, mysterious, and global,
Only one dish is the dish of dishes—
Fluffy, round, profound, delicious;

The sphere of spheres, the circled line,
The magic "O," the *fresser*'s shrine,
Jacob's ladder, King David's psalm,
A world of wisdom the size of a palm,

The source of joy and eternal spring,
Of Thee I sing ...

Latke, latke, sizzling bright
In the skillet, on that night.
Oh, what skillful hand or eye
Has shaped thy golden symmetry?

In what fragrant oil or grease
Did you rise to please, to tease
Our palate with your crunchy crust,
So soft inside, to make us lust,
To fill our hearts with an ardent passion
That can't be stilled by hamantashen!!!

The Ineffable Allure of Hamantashen

BARBARA MARIA STAFFORD

I stand before you, a humble daughter of the New Testament, where everybody has the right to salvation. It's terrifying to be called to speak about triangular pastries knowing full well that *here* not all can attain the Kingdom of Heaven.

As befits the cheerfulness of popery and the frivolity of my field, I'm going to stick to appearances. You all remember what happened when curators at the Oriental Institute strayed out of their depth and CAT-scanned a mummy. The next day the *Tribune* headlines blared: "Mummy Probed and . . . It's a Boy." Since mummies are a kind of human hamantash—lots of wrappings and a mysterious filling—I leave such dangerous hermeneutical profundities to my learned colleagues.

My topic is the ineffable allure of hamantashen, which I will epiphanically reveal with the help of bioaesthetics. Symmetry and asymmetry, gentle listeners, have long been equated with beauty or a tantalizing attractiveness. Many motor activities—walking, holding, chewing—are probably easier when features are well-matched: lips smack better, for example, when jaws are properly conjoined.

In the noble aim of demonstrating that hamantashen are not only appetizing but intrinsically alluring projectors of fascination, I've consulted Randy Thornhill's illuminating study on the role of symmetry in insect mating. Although recent, cutting-edge scientific research, aptly conducted on West Point cadets, has proven that the most symmetrical people get the most mating opportunities, the Thornhill System discovered what art historians already knew. Even in the animal world, a subtle "fluctuating symmetry" is more seductive than any mirror-image regularity. Painters have been aware of the enticements of eccentricity for a long time: Raphael's devilishly graceful madonnas, Ingres's vamps and tramps, Picasso's mistresses, reveal that curves of chin, arcs of cheek, bulges of forehead do not map exactly from the left onto the right side of the face.

But we are speaking of hamantashen attractiveness, you cry! Let's be bold. This evening I am postulating a veritable hamantashen Canon of Bewitchment. Why not? Even birds and bees like good looks. And, arguing from analogy, hamantashen possess a fiendishly irresistible shape, a sort of Geometry Pouffante, like Big Hair in Texas, making them evolutionarily selected eatable attractors. But I digress. Let us return to Thornhill's data. In his study of a West Point class, he analyzed photographs of men according to "symmetry points," mapping the centeredness of eyes, cheekbones, nose, mouth, and jaw. But I want to focus on a more prurient aspect of the test. Participants were quizzed about the age when they lost their virginity and the number of sex partners they had had since puberty (why do social scientists have all the fun?!?). Here, we must flesh out Thornhill's findings with those of Mazur, Mazur, and Keating on military rank attainment. Cutting to the chase, professional success was determined not just by physiological fitness, but by a rakish, off-center visual charm. By analogy, and extrapolating from these exciting discoveries, humans ought to prefer the slightly skewed gastronomic attractor. Luscious small mounds, not round, beckon, exuding the potent message: I want you if you want me.

Darwin, as usual, was there before Mazur, Mazur, and Keating. In his theory of natural selection, he remarks how "knobs and various fleshy appendages" (of male birds) must be attractive to females. But what, I ask, are the ornamental protuberances of the widow bird, baboon, or guppy compared to the Rubensian doughy knobs, beguiling wobbles, shifty symmetries, shadowy prune or poppy-filled pouches of hamantashen? Confident in the innate glamour of its morphology, the hamantash radiates sex appeal packaged in a sumptuous, yet compact, body. By comparison, latkes can only appear flat, minimalist, plain, uncharismatic, and this, I do believe, is the clincher—having to rely on the mere cosmetic, the maquillage of sour cream or applesauce, to disguise the fact, let's be frank, that it's just a squashed spud.

Having mentioned this deflated species, let us consider, finally and by analogy, of course, the pathetic fate of the unselected. We've all seen those *National Geographic* programs on television teaching the cruelties of evolutionary biology through visualization. All those *unchosen* males (think latkes) Darwin wrote about under the rubric of "the law of battle" (now you comprehend the appositeness of West Point!) are shown in vivid color failing to mate, languishing, dying young, getting eaten more (or less in this case). Wrenching scenes of forlorn "bachelor herds" (usually elk or moose) unfurl before our eyes, driven into melancholy madness (think latkes) while off in the radiant distance, on the most picturesque knoll of the tundra, standing tall, proud, and handsome, those *chosen* pashas (think hamantashen) disport themselves with their seraglio.

Meditating on this provocative spectacle, and following a line of argumentation I dare say wholly unknown to the gentlemen seated on this stage, I have tonight uncovered the true beauty secrets of that culinary star, the hamantash. Camille Paglia, eat your heart out!!! Conversely, we have also witnessed the appalling consequences of the latke's beauty handicap, or what happens when you just don't have that old visual magnetism.

Bull's Homage to a Latke: An Acrostic

SIMON HELLERSTEIN

Mr. Chairman, profound and distinguished colleagues, and learned guests,

No doubt you have all heard of that legendary poem, *Homage to a Latke*, written by the Literary Lion of the Latke, Jonathan Bull, in the year 1830. This singular work earned for Jonathan Bull the title of Latke Laureate—Poet Perfect of the Potato. Even today, many a lecture in literature is devoted to Bull.

It was traditional at the Oxford Hillel Latke-Hamantash Debates of the 1870s and 1880s to read Bull's *Homage to a Latke* responsively. As a fitting memorial to that literary giant, we renew that tradition this evening. Let us read responsively:

Homage to a Latke
BY JONATHAN BULL

Archly, acutely, aroused by the latke,
Busily bite into batches of latke,
    Curiously cuddle the curve of the latke,
    Dizzily dally with dishes of latke.
Eagerly eat of the essence of latke,
Fastly favor the flavor of latke.
    Gaudily garland all girths with the latke.
    Hostile to hamantash: hallow the latke.
Intensely ingest the innards of latke.
Jews: jointly enjoy the juice of the latke.
    Kugels and *knishes* kneel to the latke,
    Lovingly languid and luscious is latke.

Mystic, majestic, munificent latke,
Naiads and nymphs were nourished by latke.
> Oracles opt for the odor of latke,
> > Puritans pray for the presence of latke.
Quakers quest the quintessence of latke,
Righteous and reverent relish the latke.
> > Savour the soul of the succulent latke,
> > Toast to the taste and the tang of the latke.
Uncured are the ulcers unfed by the latke,
Voracious for victuals are vanquished by latke.
> > Wistfully wish to be wedded to latke,
> > X-tatic, X-alt, the X-emplary latke.
Youthful and yearful yearn for the latke,
Zulu and Zayde are zealous for latke.

Noshes

Though David admired Bathsheba's torso
He liked her hamantashen more so.
RALPH MARCUS, *The Lovely Triangle*

✡   ✡   ✡

A Reconstructionist latke, I submit to you, would emerge as a French crêpe, with butter instead of old lamp oil, and perhaps strawberry jam. A Reconstructionist hamantash would take the form of a chocolate log cookie, alas no more, but immortalized in my youth on 53rd Street. And as long as we can be serious, why don't we ask Manischewitz to get in touch with the Carr Water Biscuit people? We could give the matzah a new lease on our affections, a new relevance to this age of the yuppie in a yarmulke. ROGER WEISS, *Jewish Renewal*

Round Five

Combine and Deconstruct
All Ingredients

Madeleine, Oh, Madeleine; or, Meditation on Short, Plump Pastries

FRANÇOISE MELTZER

Literature has always been very interested in pastries in particular and in desserts in general. One need but remember Wallace Stevens's *The Emperor of Ice Cream*, or Proust's famous epiphany (to which we shall return shortly) to see the great extent to which the theme of dessert runs like an obsessive image throughout what we call the "canon" of literature. The fact that such a theme has been insistently ignored by literary critics until now is something which we can only lament. I shall be able today merely to touch upon this neglected area; my purpose will be a bit different. Indeed, difference—spelled, of course with an *a*—will be my main focus (difference as in deferring as well as differing, as Derrida has so often noted). I intend to look at two forms which repeatedly emerge in the myths of Western metaphysics: the circle (or latke) and the triangle (or hamantash).

In this I am, you may object, no different from anyone else on this panel. Ha! They, in the logocentric tradition that imprisons them in their post-Kantian blinder, are doomed to repeat endlessly, in Freud's sense, a *description* of these forms. For these two forms are notions which the Western tradition neither questions nor, significantly, *sees*—precisely because they are unchallenged; the unseen categories of the Western mind. A deconstruction of these two forms is what I intend to undertake here. Lest you think that I, too, am falling into the trap of those who profess to speak "the truth," those who insist on making *presence* the culmination of all discourse, let me only say that I cannot speak outside of our tradition; I too, am trapped in circles and triangles. But with the aid of the deconstructive model, I shall demonstrate that we have reached a critical point in our epistemological narrative.

Trapped, as I have already suggested, in the Kantian universe as we are, we are not only unable to discern whether, once we don green glasses, the world is green because of the glasses or just plain *green*; worse still, our ontological assumptions are such that we insist upon our myth of form. Insist—and this gathering is a mark of that insistence. For we are asked to *take sides*, to choose between one form over the other, but *never* to question the forms themselves, or indeed, the very notion of form itself. Thus this gathering participates directly in the repression of the knowledge of the extent to which this idea of "form" has invaded us, colonized our thought, and given us the illusion that, through the contrast between these two forms, *difference* is both maintained and remembered. This is the fantasy that is inscribed in Western metaphysics, and which this Tradition, this Debate, both protects and strengthens. Before I continue with my analysis, I should like to read a particularly illuminating passage from the French psychoanalyst and seminal theoretician, Jacques Lacan:

> Note that the circular figure is not first of all a figure, that is to say, imaginable, since the notion of good forms was founded on this very figure. . . . And I would go further—good form and meaning are akin. The order of meaning is naturally configured by what the form of the circle designated as the consistency presupposed to the symbolic.

I wish to say, in a type of parenthesis, that the statement just read is equally moving when read *backward*, an activity which I recently undertook. No genius for nothing, Lacan is reminding us that form is a necessary illusion, and that form *generates* meaning, and vice versa. "Good form" is not coincidentally an expression in English, then, for in "meaning" virtuous and (especially) *law abiding* behavior, it rests its case on the altar of the metaphysical prejudice we share about the idea of form itself. From the Latin *forma*, which also means "image," the notion "form" gives us the image of stability, of unchanging structures of clarity, and of difference.

Thus the attempt to choose between a latke and a hamantash is an activity which reassures us, consoles us into forgetting the gaping abyss which lies at the margins of our braille book of life. For once we deconstruct these notions, these prejudices, we discover something rather curious: these two forms, which profess to be so unlike each other, are really not different at all; they are the moment before the Hegelian sublation, the instant before the synthesis which will erase all difference in the wake of its belief in the ultimate resolution of any dialectic.

And how do we know that such is the case? How can we be sure of this (the very idea of "being sure" is itself, of course, the phallocentric insistence upon an apodictic, upon a certainty which instead marks the impossibility of same)? How, in short, can it be that the latke and the hamantash are mere orts about to merge in triumphant sublation which will neutralize the apparent dialectic? I give you the answer now and with no further ado: the answer is that the sublation of the two forms is always already present in the very existence of what we (significantly) refer to as—the croissant.

I shall give you a few moments to take in this profound and astonishing bit of information before I continue.

Let us consider the croissant for a moment. It literally means, in French, "growing." It is a present participle used in French as a noun, thus already giving substance to the notion of movement (which stands, we will agree, against that of form with all of the stasis the latter implies). When it is used as a noun in French, it first means "the waxing moon." And what does the moon wax into (or wane out of)? Why, the circle, of course. The croissant, in its endless movement toward or away from the circle, is a constant reminder of the absent presence insisting upon itself in that form. The latke stands absorbed.

Now, the croissant, it must be remembered, is only the *reminder*, as pastry, of the circle toward or away from which it strains. As a pastry, the croissant (or crescent, if you prefer) is made in three motions culminating in three "corners." Moreover, the United States, in an attempt to force the croissant more toward the hamantash than toward the latke (no doubt for dark reasons), has decided to *stuff* the croissant, much as the *taschen* of the *hamans* are stuffed. Thus the famous "croissandwich" stands as a constant memory trace of the attempt to suppress the circle, and to suppress as well the very synthesis for which the croissant always already stands.

Indeed, suppression lies at the heart of the croissant's history. What is suppressed by the French is that the pastry croissant was invented by the Viennese, and not the French at all. The Austrians invented it ostensibly to commemorate the Austrian victory over the Turks in 1689. In fact, however, this was a repressed explanation in itself, for the real reason for the invention of the croissant in Vienna is, quite simply, as a collective unconscious prefiguration of the man who uncovered repression and who was born in Vienna (not in that order): Sigmund Freud. Further, this official Austrian explanation of the birth of the croissant from a military victory strains to put the croissant (*Hornchen* in German) in the camp of the hamantash, thus suppressing the circle once again. Finally, the croissant as a Muslim emblem is always at odds with another form (which we shall consciously repress for now): the cross. The equivalent of the Red Cross in Muslim countries is the Croissant Rouge, clearly a repression of the cross and the triumph of the Turkish flag.

But the most astonishing repression of the croissant form and its implications comes from one of the greatest passages in world (yes, world) literature: the moment of the tea and madeleine in Proust's *Remembrance of Things Past*. The narrator, it will be recalled, eats a bit of a madeleine which he has dunked in some tea, and his involuntary memory (needing nothing more than this precise combination) really "goes to town" as we say, and rediscovers the whole of the narrator's childhood in the small town of Combray. Now, the question is, why does the great Proust choose a madeleine pastry to describe this epiphany, and not a croissant? Is this merely a terrible mistake?

If one looks at the text (and one does, in literary criticism, look at the text, in despair, when all else fails), one discovers that Proust describes the madeleine in the following terms: "one of those short, plump little cakes called petites madeleines which look as though they had been molded in the fluted scallop of a pilgrim's shell." A close reading of this text will uncover a subtext, in which we find another word inscribed: croissant. How is this so?

Well . . . the first words used to describe the madeleine are the same that could be used to depict a croissant: a short, plump little dessert (I have excised the word "cakes" which Proust uses because I feel that it confuses my argument here). The only thing that distinguishes the madeleine from the croissant is the fact that the former is shell-shaped (yet another form, the deep structure of which I shall today elide), so named because the pilgrims used to hold out Saint John shells for alms. And of what pilgrims are we speaking? Are we referring here to the American pilgrims (the time would be apt, of course) and their turkeys? No. No, again. We, or rather Proust, is referring to the pilgrims of the Crusades. Aha! The word "crusade" is, needless to say, a deformation of the word *croisade*, the *crois* of which, meaning cross, is the same as the *crois* in croissant, meaning crescent. And who fought in the Crusades? The Crescent fought against the Cross, of course, so the word "croissant" already insists upon a Turkish defeat—it colonizes the crescent. Thus we can see that Proust uses the pastry "petite madeleine" or madeleine as an oblique allusion to the *croissant* and to its history in the Holy Land. From a literary-psychoanalytical view, we may say that the allusion is oblique because Proust only unconsciously alludes to this. Given that he had a Jewish mother and a Catholic father, it is no surprise that Proust's allusion to the croissant is indirect, for it is, finally, an allusion to the conflict within him, the very exterior homeland of which was the locus of the clash between crosses and crescents.

So in conclusion, our literary approach to this issue has led us to affirm the following: the croissant is the conflation of the hamantash and the latke. And the croissant itself is a further synthesis of the crescent and the cross. The "croissandwich" is a backformation to the hamantash. The madeleine, with its biblical and Crusade-like allusions, is a croissant manqué. The latke is a moon about to wane, and therefore also a croissant.

Now that we have seen how everything is really everything else in the Western logos, and how the dialectic is always subverted, it is only left for me to remind you what Lacan says: form and meaning are always joined. Function follows form. Your choice of food for breakfast, for example—whether it be French toast, pancakes, latkes, bagels, hamantashen, English muffins, or sticky buns—this choice is not an innocent one, nor is it ever merely fun or random. It is a serious, grim affair. Moreover, if you make the effort, you will see that there is a close (indeed, symbiotic) relation between the pastry you choose and the books you read. Tell me what you eat, and I'll tell you what you read. For the deep structure will be the same, and the symptom, therefore, expressed in form. In short, the notion of "textuality" must be read also to mean the way in which the subject inscribes himself upon his morning pastry. Only then can the full political thrust of any text be freed from its logocentric base, its phallocentric bias, and the oppressive force of form over taste.

The Hermeneutics of the Hamantash

EMILIE S. PASSOW

I will be brief, laconic, lucid, modest, accessible and engaging, as scholars tend to be. Witty in style, wise in content—the implied duality here an unfortunate consequence of the nonsimultaneity of language rather than any deliberate regression to prepostmodern Cartesian dualism, my discussion will be definitive. Inadequate as it is to the referent of the hamantash, I will dispense with the oppressive referential of patriarchal linear logic and deploy the cogency of lyricism as well as conceptual syncopation to signal my post-poststructuralist work of undermining the deconstruction of meaning within a *gantze megillah* framework. My argument will reappropriate any cultural, historical, social, ethnic, seasonal, geometric, and culinary privilege from the latke to the hamantash, where it appropriately belongs. In short, I will be direct yet indeterminate, without prejudice to diversity.

Etymologically, the term "hamantash" or "hamantasche" is Teutonic in origin, despite the Persian etiology of the occasion. (Recent history, in fact, has demonstrated a common Aryan claim, especially in the proclivity to genocide.) *Tasche*, of course, is a Germanic noun signifying "bag," in this context, an implicit metaphor for "container" in several modes or guises. Structurally, the dough contains the filling as a soft, secure pouch. Psychologically, as maladaptive ego defense mechanisms rooted in unresolved Oedipal conflicts, vanity and the lust for power entrap Haman's potential for authentic, caring self-realization, again as the dough encloses the filling of the hamantash. Simultaneously an emblem of protection and destruction, the hamantash, then, is a paradigm of deconstructive literary strategies and the sociology of scapegoating. As such, however, the hermeneutics of the hamantash ironically transform the biblical lament of Ecclesiastics, that "all is vanity," into the metaconceit that "all is Wissenschaft."

Supplementing this universal subjectivity are the hamantash's unique dimensionality, materiality, and intertextuality. Similarly, its confluence of visual, aromatic, and oral pleasures generates pregnant pause. Poppy or prune, cherry, blueberry, honey or apricot, its rainbow centers add seductive color to the demure ivory dough. With its crumbly crust and smooth marmalade, a happy hamantash makes a happy meal, not to mention how it reconciles existential opposites, a Jewish yin/yang, one might say.

From a spatial-typological angle, the hamantash challenges easy formulaic transposition of area or volume. When properly pinched, after all, the equilateral sides are arched, reminding us of the roundness of space and the insouciance of nonsense. (This feature is well documented in children's folklore. See "My Hat, It Has Three Corners" in the *Journal of the American Jewish Historical Society*.)

From a temporal perspective, the hamantash requires more time, more concentration, and more skill to be first sculpted, then savored, then swallowed and digested than does the flat, unprofitable, colorless pastiche of eggs and potatoes known as the potato pancake and pretentiously dubbed the "latke" only to lend it an aristocratic aura and an ethnic flavor.

A function of both the quality of the baker's artistry and the eater's appreciation, the longer interval required to make and break the hamantash, so to speak, overrides the technological conveniences available to shred and mix the pedestrian ingredients of the latke.

Indeed, aesthetically, the hamantash incorporates more elements of a robust creative process than does the lame latke. Simply compare and contrast these elegant steps necessary to mold a hamantash with the messy ones implicated in preparing the latke: to gather (the flour, eggs, water, oil, and sugar), to knead, to shape, and to fill with ... to peel, to putter, and to fry.

Aurally speaking, the hamantash bakes in silence akin to the workings of the mysteries of the universe: light, gravity, consciousness. In other words, the hamantash is no less than an objective correlative for the unbearable lightness of being.

Transcending the unbearable lightness of being, we reach the theological. Within Judaic perimeters, the triangular formation of the hamantash signifies the tripartite partnership in Creation among God, nature, and humanity. This noble endeavor we call *tikkun olam*, the repair of the world, in which *everyone* can participate, symbolically rather than transubstantially, by eating the hamantash.

Thus so ends this hermeneutic of the hamantash, in the kitchen, where we belong.

Noshes

As we all know from Women's Studies 101, those in power define and the powerless are defined. As women we are defined by men as the makers of *knishes*, *blintzes*, latkes, and hamantashen. As can be seen from a history of these debates, male experts have produced the knowledge about women's work. Just as there have been male medical experts defining the childbirth experience for women, there are male gastronomic experts defining women's experience in the kitchen. For years we have accepted the patriarchal definitions, and our own voices and experiences have been silenced.

This point is illustrated by the brilliant feminist short story, "I'm Not Hungry; I Had a Bite to Eat in the Kitchen," the only writing produced by an anonymous maker of latkes. MARIAMNE H. WHATLEY, *A Feminist Perspective on the Latke-Hamantash Debate*

✡   ✡   ✡

After all, what is a hamantash? A three-cornered pastry, it has no single property which characterizes it, but rather like the pluralism Horace Kallen hoped for in a liberalized America, it derives its essence from the distinctiveness of its parts. It is made up of two equal sections—the crust and the filling—neither of which has to give up anything in order to be part of the whole. Unlike latkes, the symbol of the melting pot with its narrow definition of American identity, the hamantash does not require people to subject themselves to meltdown nor does it force them to have their cultures and customs beaten out of them and amalgamated in a bowl or frying pan. Rather, it offers a culinary/cultural metaphor of gently wrapping the dough of America around an almost infinite array of fillings, and thus proving that diversity can be folded into the American system without surrendering integrity and authenticity.

When Frederick Bartholdi cast about for an appropriate symbol for America's liberty, he opted for a symbol of a hamantash. The torch of the Statue of Liberty clearly represents the tip of the hamantash, while the slightly open space in the middle corresponds to the statue's face, and her feet parallel the hamantash's base. So too Emma Lazarus in her winning poem, "The New Colossus," echoed the rejection of the homogenous latke as too limited as a model for America. Her reference to the "huddled masses" no doubt are the fillings inside the hamantash, peering from their window of dough, "yearning to breathe free." HASIA DINER, *The Latke, the Hamantash, and the Struggle for a Symbol of the American National Character*

Round Six

Semiotics
and Anti-Semiotics

Heartburn as a Cultural System

MICHAEL SILVERSTEIN

To all who have experienced it *fun heym aroys* ("one from the hearth"), Jewish food is no laughing matter. It is not so much belly laugh as bellyache, a kind of hearth-burn, as it were. It could not be by chance that the English translation of the letters on the *dreidl*, the Khanuke top, spells out T-U-M-S. God may play dice with the universe, but not with Mrs. Schmalowitz's *lukshn kugl*, nor especially with her latkes and homntashen. It is not my purpose merely to offer native exegesis of the two culinary heroes of the hours, the latke and the homntash. The real heroes are Sol Tax, my colleague in social anthropology—*zol er derleybn iber hundert un tsvantsig yor* ("may he live to be a hundred and twenty years")—and the late Louis Gottschalk, who thirty-nine years ago set an impossible task: to debate the merits or, later when it had become clear that neither side could possibly win, to explain the significance, of the latke on the one hand, and of the homntash on the other. Indeed, there may have been something of the totemistic involved, a kind of starchy moiety system, perhaps exophagous, though I would not speculate on who thought he was from the latke moiety and who from the homntash. It appears that Sol was very wise in putting forward only these two important items, so as to test our insights as well as our insides with a perennial ethnogustatory problem that requires an ingenious dietary supplement to solve this brain teaser in the medium of brain food, a Sphinx-like riddle truly worthy of and fit for an Edible Rex.

For what are these two culinary symbols but the two central elements of the gustemic code. They are two words of a larger silent discourse—remember what your *tate-mame* told you, don't talk when your mouth is full—a cultural text with its food in its mouth, waiting for us, as good structuralists and semioticians, to read it. To read, perchance to savor, the eloquent simplicity of the code when viewed in its proper, four-part totality.

The riddle of the latke and the homntash can never be "solved" as such, as it were, until these two are viewed as gustemes of a gustemic poetry or music that is full of sound and fury—at least of prune filling—but that signifies nothing if not heard in its textual plenitude, which we must deconstruct before we can digest. With all due respect to my learned colleagues here assembled, arguing over the priority of invention, or using external criteria of worth, are clearly just the most subjective and unconvincing of partisan strategies. No, once you've caught a code, you've seized the germ of the system of symbols, only in terms of which can any symbol's meaning be understood. It is an edible logic of—if you're not careful with the dough—the concrete.

So let us look—*lomir khapn a kuk*—at how Jewish cuisine plays variations on a theme of farina, using the latke and the homntash as gustemic notes of the harmonious syntax of the yearly liturgical cycle. (The bagel and bialy, because they are rather fishy under the best of circumstances, need not be adduced to demonstrate that the [w]hole determines some of its parts.)

Kukt ir shoyn oif, khaveyrim, observe, then, the inexorable logic of the system, as shown in figure 1. By arranging the gustemic symbols according to the calendric order of festivals of which they are particularly characteristic, we see immediately that the latke is a real operator. A bit of symbolic analysis, maestro! The latke's circumference outlines the path of the edges of the spinning *dreidl* with which it is associated in its season, and so ranges from circular to ellipsoid in shape. In confirmation, we note that this is also the projection onto a plane of a potato, of an onion, or of an egg, its ingredients. Let us play Spin the Latke through the yearly cycle. What are the characteristic foods of the year?

First, at Rosh Hashone, the characteristic food is *teyglekh*, little spherical pellets of dough that are browned and boiled in honey, a brown sweet, and then piled high, ideally into the form of a pyramid, where it forms a sweet gooey mass that must have confused the ancient pharaohs into thinking that the Jews were particularly good at architecture. The brown honeyed matrix, outside and around the

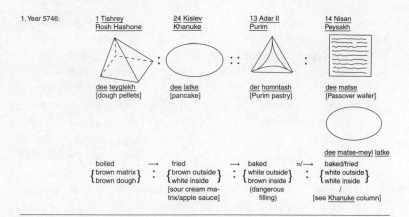

FIGURE 1

balls, holds the construction together. (I should point out the parallel in the weekly gustemic symbology of *knaydlekh* in a bowl of chicken soup.)

Now let us turn to the latke, that flat, oval construction of potato and onion, held together by a gooey matrix of egg. It is fried in oil until it is brown on the outside and white on the inside. Observe— whether you're observant, as they say, or not—that this relatively flattened circularity is the projection of the sphere on a two-dimensional surface, as we noted already *en passant*. So note that we have moved from a relatively three-dimensional object, to a two-dimensional one, in a mental operation of constructing the ideal, the conceptual latke, as we might term it. Taken together, these two items form a kind of ur-paradigm of the Jewish calendric food chain, moving from Tishrei to Kislev, or perhaps from Minsk to Pinsk, in about eighty days.

Now what is remarkable is that the last part of the gustatory cycle is clearly formed from the intersection of these two primordial or simplex gustemes, moving the year to its more complex phase. The last two symbols illustrate the gustemic complex, even though they may be psychologically healthier. For we see that both the homntash and the matse fit into a gustemically logical discourse that shows both the symmetry of repetition and the asymmetry of transformation.

Six months after *teyglekh* (and Tashlikh) come homntashen, once more three-dimensional objects formed, interestingly, from laying the conceptual latke on a gooey triangular surface of the original pyramidal shape. And here I should point out the interesting variant transformations, involved, no doubt, with the masking of the true nature of the symbolic logic. As shown in figure 2, either we can inscribe a circle in the triangular surface of the pyramid, yielding figure 2a, which might also be confused with the taboo *eyn horeh*, the evil eye, that stares at us from the back of the almighty dollar, as Max Weber would point out about the Protestant ethic—or, more cleverly, we can inscribe the triangular surface of the *teyglekh* pyramid in the latke circle, or ellipse, in which case we also have enough dough left over to fold the edges up, forming the chords and arcs shown on the finished homntash, moving from 2b to the homntash column of figure 1.

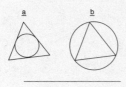

FIGURE 2

Ikh makh shoyn nisht keyn lange megillah—it needs no long story to see that the homntash, filled with one of two physiologically dangerous brown substances, is both a repeat, at the complex gustemic level, of the *teyglekh* pyramid enhanced by the latke concept, and at the same time is a substantial inversion of the precious point of the year, the latke. The homntash is browned from baking, then relatively light or white in the substance of the outside or doughy material, and filled with dark brown on the inside. This is inverse to the latke, which is smothered in *smetene*, white sour cream, surface-browned through frying, and white in the substance of the interior-most batter. For those of you who want a *pareve* symbol, one that can be eaten with meat, note the transformation into *pommes*—applesauce—and *pommes de terre* (apples of the earth, or potatoes), which clearly substitutes for the light or white outside gooey variable in the symbolic construction of the latke, but preserves its structural integrity. This is clearly a reference to the Garden of Eden, but we will not digress on biblical interpretation here.)

Finally, as you can see clearly in figure 3, when we inscribe a horizontal cross-section of the *teyglekh* pyramid in the latke, conceptually truncating the *teyglekh* pyramid by a crossed latke plane, we generate the square, or its close approximation, which follows quickly on Haman's heels in Nisan, as though pursued and delivered from an enemy, *a finstere yor oif zey*, may they suffer dark years. The matse, again a two-dimensional correspondent to the three-dimensional homntash, is both white on the outside and white on the inside, exactly the inverse of the *teyglekh*. It's also very, very dry. It should be noted that the matse-meyl latke, the optional variant that adds complexity to the Peysakh gusteme, consists of the repetition of the latke, only complexly built from a material that is in its underlying structure the crumbled and pulverized matse itself, thus confirming the correctness of this analysis by having the latke come up on us again, as it were.

This whole process of conceptual transformation through gustemic discourse takes less than eight months (or nine in leap years), leaving the other four or five no doubt to recuperate. But anyone who has eaten fully of these symbols needs no such explanation.

I must insist then that in posing the riddle of the latke and the homntash our colleagues were cleverly posing the question of why the latke and the homntash are the mediating elements of the gustemic discourse, which role can easily now be seen from their interior position in the quadripartite metrics of the gustemic year. They allow us to transform the *teyglekh* at the yearly renewal of God's covenant into the matse at the deliverance from enemies. Jewish symbols, however, are not just good to think; they are also good to eat. And you don't have to be Jewish to enjoy Lévi-Strauss's Talmudic cuisine.

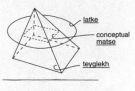

FIGURE 3

Latke vs. Hamantash: A Feminist Critique

JUDITH SHAPIRO

My own moment of enlightenment about the significance of latkes and hamantashen came one day after many hours of studying a genealogical diagram of the kind anthropologists have traditionally used for making the study of kinship incomprehensible. In such diagrams, which represent relationships of descent, siblingship, and marriage, triangles are used to represent males and circles to represent females.

"Why should this be so?" I suddenly asked myself in one of those great moments in an academic career when you rise above your limiting assumptions and see your life's work for the arbitrary *mishegass* it really is. But are we in fact dealing with arbitrariness here? Are these triangles and circles truly arbitrary "symbols" in the Peircian sense of the term "symbol"? Or are they rather "icons," that is, signs that bear a material resemblance to what they represent? Are they not motivated, rather than arbitrary, signs? And, if so, what is the nature of that motivation?

Upon reflection, it became clear that the triangles and the circles were indubitably iconic representations of hamantashen and latkes respectively, and, moreover, that hamantashen were representations of men and latkes of women.

Or was it the reverse? That is, were men representations of hamantashen and women representations of latkes? Although the resolution of this issue might have seemed self-evident in prepostmodern times, we are now able to see the matter in its full complexity, ambiguity, intertextuality, decenteredness, and infinite regression.

The surprising reversibility of sign and referent, with all of its antifoundational implications, is something that anthropologists commonly experience in the course of their fieldwork. For example, a colleague of mine reports that the Mehinaku of the Upper Xingu region of central Brazil believe that if a man dreams of having an erection, it means he is in danger of encountering a snake when he goes hunting the following day. (That happens to be an authentic ethnographic fact, incidentally.)

All of which leads me to conclude that it is ultimately impossible for us to know whether, in the last analysis, the latke and hamantash should be seen as semiotic representations of the two sexes or whether the two sexes should be seen as semiotic representations of latkes and hamantashen. What is not, however, in doubt, is the association of latkes with the female principle and hamantashen with the male.

Sociolinguistic evidence clearly bears this out. We need take only the example of the speech event in which we are currently engaged. Now, it is a fact that throughout the history of the Latke-Hamantash Debate, *until this evening,* the opposing terms always and invariably appear in the same order: "latke-hamantash," not "hamantash-latke." The reason is that we say "latke and hamantash" just as we say "ladies and gentlemen." A moment's thought will suffice to make you realize that the reverse is also true, a phenomenon that I have already had occasion to analyze above.

It is hard to know what to make of the reversal of the tradition that we see on the flyer for tonight's debate: hamantash-latke. Is it a feminist tactic to raise our consciousness about the traditional unmarked order of these terms, as a preparation for showing that the apparent priority given to the female term is an illusion, a cynical placing of latkes on an apparent pedestal? Or is it just sexism pure and simple? I am not yet prepared to answer that question, since it clearly requires further research and reflection.

At this point, it becomes necessary for me to address counterarguments to the position I am developing here, as transparently misguided and foolish as these counterarguments may be. I have, for example, heard it asserted that the triangle (and thus the hamantash) can be seen as a female symbol of some kind or other. Surely this is too sophisticated an audience to require any extended critique of such a vulgar materialist bio-corporeal-reductionist approach to gender. In any event, Freud definitively disposed of such interpretations of the hamantash in his classic analysis of Irma's dream of the *knish*.

Which brings us to the question of how post-Freudian psychoanalytical approaches to gender bear upon the latke/hamantash question. I am thinking in particular of Jacques Lacan's early and influential paper, "Prolegomenon toward an etherealized and obscurantist view of gender and sexuality," in which he first develops his theory of the latke as "lack": an absent signifier that is yet too heavy to be free-floating. While some feminist scholars have considered Lacan's work an important advance over earlier Freudian theories of female sexuality, most notably Freud's idea that women have babies as a symbolic substitute for having hamantashen, some of us see it as the same old prune filling, and we know what that's a symbol for.

In fact, we would do well to leave the field of psychoanalysis altogether for the more fertile terrain of cultural anthropology and comparative social history if we wish to find the most convincing evidence for the gender symbolism inherent in latkes and hamantashen. The cross-cultural record is particularly clear on the association of the hamantash, that is the triangle, or the triad, with masculinity. The patriarchal Christian trinity is an example familiar to all of us. I could also give you numerous examples from other, more exotic societies in different parts of the world, the beauty of such examples being that you would probably not be in any position to question the accuracy either of my data or my analysis. But I will resist that temptation this evening, situating the latke and hamantash instead within their own cultural tradition, one with which most of us have at least a passing familiarity, perhaps too passing for some of our older relatives.

Let us contemplate the obvious significance of the hamantash as a symbol—or, rather, to be analytically precise, an indexical sign—of Haman. Here there is some debate as to its precise meaning. Some of us were brought up thinking that it represents Haman's three-cornered hat. In Hebrew, however, the term for hamantash translates as "Haman's ears," therefore presenting us with an instance of somatic, as opposed to sartorial, indexicality (cf. Barthes 1965; Baudrillard 1987). Yet another interpretation is suggested by the meaning of the term *tash*, or *tasche*, as "purse" or "handbag"; was Haman perhaps a transvestite, and was his aggressive machismo then a form of overcompensation for his secret longing to be a woman? Is this, in fact, the root of his demented hostility toward Queen Esther? Was he secretly jealous of her wardrobe?

Be this as it may, it remains evident that the hamantash represents the Judaic tradition in its vengeful patriarchal mode. How can we forget the song we learned to sing as children:

For Haman he was swinging while Mordecai was singing
In Shu-Shu-Shu-shan long ago.

Is this the aspect of Judaic tradition that brought us to these nice Quaker institutions? And when we eat hamantashen, do we not, moreover, perpetuate an unhealthy identification with the oppressor along the lines so compellingly set forth in Fanon's work on the psychology of colonialism? (I should note that I am departing here from the traditional interpretation of the eating of hamantashen as a form of metonymic cannibalistic incorporation of the enemy, which is of course just the sort of interpretation you would expect from a scholarly establishment that is itself vengeful and patriarchal, not to mention cannibalistic.)

If we wish instead to draw upon the more authentic Jewish tradition of identification with the oppressed, and to assert our identity as members of an academic community, in which, as the familiar expression goes, many of our best Jews are Friendish, it is the latke and not the hamantash that must command our allegiance. In making this choice, we acknowledge the essential—and at the same time essentialist—contribution that Judaism and feminism together have made to the Quaker tradition.

Now, while I would not wish to stir up a two-college rivalry on this occasion, I feel I must point out that Bryn Mawr has a longer history than Haverford does of recognizing the moral significance of the latke. What, after all, are such rituals as circular dancing around the maypole and the hoop race down senior row otherwise about?

I hasten to add, however, that while Haverford has come to latke consciousness more recently, it is not only about to catch up with but about to surpass Bryn Mawr. I am hoping to demonstrate this in a work currently in progress, which is tentatively entitled "Latke Symbolism as a Key to Understanding the Changing Focus of the Haverford Diversity Requirement." While I do not have time now to go into the details of the arguments I am developing in that work, I would just note the central theme, which concerns the transformation of the latke from a metaphor of the generalized Other to a metonym of social justice.

I close, then, with a question for all of us: is it not time—long past time, in fact—to leave behind the hamantash of Haman in order to embrace the latke of Queen Esther?

Latke vs. Hamantash: A Materialist-Feminist Analysis; A Reply to Judith Shapiro

ROBIN LEIDNER

Professor Judith Shapiro has made an invaluable contribution to scholarship by bringing the insights of feminist and postmodern theory to bear on the interpretation of Jewish foodstuffs. It is surely no coincidence that shortly after the appearance of this paper, Professor Shapiro, who had been serving as provost of a provincial women's college in an obscure Philadelphia suburb, was chosen to become president of Barnard College in New York. The usefulness of this learned, stimulating, highly original paper is hampered only by its complete wrongheadedness. This forum is an ideal setting for a frank reappraisal, since Professor Shapiro's departure from the vicinity allows us to focus on her faulty logic and inadequate methodology without fear of contradiction.

To summarize briefly an account that is richly nuanced (in fact, often incomprehensibly convoluted), Shapiro, an anthropologist, begins with the conjecture that the circles and triangles conventionally used to designate women and men on kinship charts are in fact iconic representations of latkes and hamantashen. She argues, "(I)t is ultimately impossible for us to know whether, in the last analysis, the latke and hamantash should be considered as semiotic representations of the two sexes or whether the two sexes should be seen as semiotic representations of latkes and hamantashen. What is not, however, in doubt, is the association of latkes with the female principle and hamantashen with the male" (Shapiro, 117).

What is it that leads Shapiro to argue as a feminist that latkes, which have so clearly been part of the oppressive apparatus upholding the most retrograde patriarchal elements of Judaism, are a more appropriate symbol for women than hamantashen? I will argue that such an interpretation is possible only if analysis remains at a symbolic level which so decontextualizes the subject that there is no trace of the lived experience of the relevant social actors. In short, I will argue that this mistaken assertion is a product of the pernicious poststructuralist *mishegass* that has, in discipline after discipline, tempted scholars to abandon their investigations of the physical and social world in order to concentrate on a world of discourse that takes on greater importance, indeed greater reality. In the interests of defending sociology from the forces that have desiccated anthropology, history, literary criticism, cultural studies, and other pretenders to knowledge of the social world, I will argue that a clear understanding of the gendered implications of latkes and hamantashen must rest on careful empirical research. I will demonstrate definitively that attention to culturo-linguistic-symbolic content is illuminating only in conjunction with rigorous investigation of the material conditions under which the objects of analysis are produced and consumed.

I have conducted extensive participant observation over many years of the production and consumption of both latkes and hamantashen. Based on my fieldwork and on in-depth interviews with non-market-oriented Jewish cooks, I will demonstrate that when one takes into account the gendered division of labor, family power dynamics, norms of sociability, and the structural conditions of participation in a late-capitalist, postindustrial economy, the hamantash is far more suitable for incorporation into the feminist vision of an egalitarian and nonoppressive future than is the latke.

Let us turn first to the latke. The material conditions of latke production are stressed in the best-known analysis of the latke as a factor in the oppression of women, Emma Goldman's famous "blood of our foremothers" speech. In it, she asked, "How much of the very blood of our foremothers' knuckles have we battered and fattened on every Hanukkah, for surely their lifeblood is invariably an ingredient in our latkes? Could oceans of applesauce or mountains of sour cream ever fully mask the salty taste of the tears of our onion-grating sisters?" More than fifty years after Goldman's death, these questions still haunt us.

Time limits prevent me from quoting many of the moving accounts that my interviewees provided of what their Hanukkahs are like. But put yourself in the position of these women (for it is of course women who produce the latkes in the great majority of households). The children are overexcited and rambunctious. Perhaps guests are expected. Much of the holiday meal has already been prepared, but the cook feels obliged to provide fresh latkes, not reheated ones. After peeling, grating, frying batch after batch in spitting oil, the cook is exhausted and sweaty, her hair hangs in greasy clumps, her knuckles are scraped raw, her arms sting from the continual splatters of oil. When at last a heaping plate of latkes is ready, she brings it to the table, where every one is snatched up immediately. Stoically, she heads back to the stove to begin frying the next batch. From the dining room drift peals of laughter, snatches of conversation, the splat of applesauce, and shouted inquiries about when the latkes will be ready. Excluded from the community, she spends most of the holiday meal on her feet in front of the hot stove, forcing a gay smile during her brief forays to deliver latkes. Her labor does not end with the meal, for back in the kitchen potato peels are overflowing the garbage can, numerous bowls and utensils wear a thick layer of potato mixture, now disagreeably blackened, and of course a sticky film of grease covers all exposed surfaces. Despite her best efforts, the smell, having permeated the drapes, will linger for weeks.

No doubt many of you are now thinking of the same thing: Cuisinarts. It is certainly true that some of the more dangerous and painful labor involved in latke production has been reduced by technological developments, and survey research by Tsimmes and Tsurris (1993) confirms that Cuisinart ownership is a significant factor in explaining variation in the degree of resentment among latke-makers. Yet I maintain that only those who benefit from the subordination of women, or those bamboozled by a deeply entrenched system of mystification, could argue that latke-production is now "a piece of cake."

In fact, the impact of the Cuisinart on women's position in Judaism has been quite limited. Following the familiar pattern of many so-called household conveniences, the Cuisinart has increased demand for latkes and generated increasingly fussy standards of latke texture without changing the power dynamics that are really at issue here. (I don't think that I need even elaborate on the classism of commentators who overlook the reality that access to Cuisinarts is highly class-stratified.) Another modern development, the marketing of prepared latke mixes, has had even less effect on the overall picture. Such mixes are their own punishment, and judging from my sample they are never purchased more than once.

Content analysis of my interview data shows that a few themes dominate the cooks' accounts: physical suffering, pressure, and social isolation.

The picture for hamantashen is very different. First, for many of my informants, the home has ceased to be a site of hamantash production. Such households calculate that the cost of the time, effort, and skill of household members outweighs the cost of store-bought hamantashen and the diminished quality of the product. In the capitalist marketplace, the hamantash is reduced to a commodity like any other, and we should not be surprised that capitalist competition has led to the year-round availability of neohamantashen with alien fillings, their brightly colored jams signaling their debasement to the level of the workaday Danish.

Nevertheless, many of my respondents and their families and friends do reserve hamantash consumption for Purim, and some apparently deem mass-produced commercial hamantashen an unacceptable substitute for the infinitely more delicious and not very hard to make home-baked hamantashen that can be produced with my no-yeast recipe (see page 203).

Certainly the happiest households are those where hamantash production takes place at home, usually as a collective enterprise. A special time is set aside for unhurried hamantash activity, in contrast to the high-pressure time crunch we saw in the case of latkes. In general, several household members cooperate in the production of hamantashen. Some disagreeable work has been marketized, because feminist pressure has led to the development of a substitute for home-made fillings that is not only acceptable, but preferable: prune butter, or *lekvar*, purchased by the jar. The scene is one of mutual enjoyment, as children, their faces smeared with *lekvar*, help cut out circles of dough; older members of the household guide their efforts and praise their helpfulness; participants are often moved to sing; a wonderful aroma fills the home. Everyone is permitted to sample the hamantashen as they emerge from the oven, newly plump and warm. It is true that flour is all over everything, but cleanup is eased by the cheerful cooperation of older children and adults.

The themes that emerged most often from my interviews about hamantashen were: fun, nostalgia, and togetherness.

For women, it is clear that hamantashen offer far more scope for self-realization, egalitarian relations, and social progress than do latkes. The liberating potential of the hamantash is especially great because Purim provides a clear model of a feminist heroine in the Megillah (the Purim scroll). I speak, of course, of Vashti, who bravely resisted patriarchal authority (reinforced by state power) and refused to accept the powerless position of the trophy wife exhibited as an ego-booting *tchatchke* at her husband's command. I don't think we need go as far as some critics do in describing Esther as a "male-identified scab" in order to acknowledge that it is Vashti whose independence, personal integrity, and brave refusal to be judged according to male standards are more worthy of celebration.

Could latkes ever be a force for the empowerment of women? My most recent field notes suggest that, given the right objective conditions, latkes could provoke in the masses of Jewish women the kind of revolutionary fervor that they triggered in Emma Goldman. It is those years, when women have to start in with the latkes before they've recovered from Thanksgiving, that have the most revolutionary potential. In such times, many women pierce the false consciousness that has contributed to their subordination; indeed, much of the language of the transcripts from this year's interviews is unprintable. We must start laying the groundwork now if we are to be ready the next year Hanukkah falls early, ready for revolutionary change brought about by the determined unity of Jewish women and the support of enlightened men. The revolution need not abolish latkes, but must abolish the gendering of burdensome holiday labor so that it may be shared. Interfaith marriage might help create a vanguard for this movement. Are Jewish husbands of non-Jewish wives taking responsibility for their own latkes? If so, could that provoke a generalized loosening of gendered latke norms? I plan to pursue these questions in future research.

Some critics have suggested that my unflinching analysis of the material conditions of latke production could play into the hands of the virulent anti-Semitic fringe groups in Idaho, which might interpret my arguments as part of a larger Jewish conspiracy to control their state's potato-based economy. While I believe that we need not stifle debate within the Jewish community out of fear, I do take this concern seriously. I have been careful to avoid language that could be construed as tuberphobic, and trust that our community can sustain a candid and vigorous discussion that will avoid descending to *ad potatum* attacks.

Just as I do not reject the potato, I do not object to the inclusion of some analysis of the symbolic content of latkes and hamantashen in determining their feminist potential. Had Shapiro grounded her cultural analysis in investigation of the everyday realities of production and consumption, she surely would not have come so close to accepting an essentialist view of gender, as she appears to in speaking of a purported "association of latkes with the female principle and hamantashen with the male."

Feminist scholars have demonstrated again and again that gender categories are malleable and that variation within genders is virtually always greater than average differences between genders. The hamantash is a perfect representation of this more flexible, culturally variable, view of gender. For while the hamantash begins as a circle (which Shapiro tags female), it becomes a triangle through conscious human intervention, without ever losing its qualities of circularity. The hamantash is an inspiring demonstration of the possibilities of overcoming essentialist dualisms: without the circle, there could be no triangle, and without the triangle, the circle would be empty. The hamantash provides a vision of human possibility that similarly integrates the strengths that have been attributed to men and women. I leave you with the hope that some day we all can achieve that blending of circle and triangle, the synthesis of smoothness and crunch, the simultaneous embodiment of openness and fullness that we find in the hamantash.

Latkes and Hamantashen as Dominant Symbols in Jewish Critical Thought

MARVIN MIRSKY

The latke is relatively flat and approximately round—the flatter and rounder, the nearer to what Plato might have called the "form" or "idea" of latke. It has been grossly referred to as a potato pancake, but this canard fails to account for the magical transmutation that occurs to the potato during the latke-making process. In contrast, the hamantash may be visualized as a three-cornered hat with a peak in the center or, alternatively, as a depressed three-sided pyramid with seams. It is made of dough that, after baking, usually retains its original consistency, and it is filled with black grains of sand which, it is claimed, are edible.

Scholarly impartiality forbids my expressing, or even implying, any preference between these two symbols, as rich in nourishment as in meaning. It remains only for us to examine the meaning of these symbols—the dominant symbols in Jewish history and, perforce, in Jewish critical thought.

Reference to the physical appearance of these symbols may prove helpful; at the same time, a limited analogy with Platonic and Aristotelian thought conceived as two poles of the philosophic spectrum may not be without value. Thus, the roundness of the latke clearly suggests the circle of perfection (Plato's ideal form), the endlessness of eternity ("in my beginning is my end," "world without end," etc.); while the flatness of the latke, having eliminated all distinguishing prominences and peaks of particularity, emphasizes the general and the universal (Plato's ultimate truth beyond the illusion of the immediate and the particular).

In contrast, the triangularity of the hamantash suggests balance and limitation (Aristotle's "mean" between excess and deficiency); its angularity emphasizes the immediate and particular; and its content (black sand) reminds us of the earth (the real rather than the ideal).

What, you may ask, is the connection between this conflict and the subject of this evening's debate: the Latke, the Hamantash, and the Generational Gap? The answer is evident. Both the symbols and the gap represent a fundamental polarization of human attitudes, a polarization that all too often is reflected in the formation of antipathetic groups. With only the slightest adaptation, these symbols can readily be extended to embrace the eternal conflict between the generations—age vs. youth, tradition vs. novelty, teacher vs. students, and so on. The only problem would seem to be: who is the latke, who the hamantash?

The Hamantash vs. the Latke:
An Archetypal Study

EUGENE GOODHEART

The hamantash is one of the most significant instances of the archetype. With its triangular shape (equilateral triangle in its archetypal form) and its sweet prune inside, the hamantash embodies
some of the deepest values of Western civilization and for all I know
of Eastern civilization as well. The triangle, the trinity (father, son,
and the holy ghost): the archetype, with its peculiar capacity for
identification, interfusion, and confusion, embraces all religions. Beginning as a symbol of the Jewish struggle for freedom, the hamantash, in its inescapable triangularity, acquired its Christian aspect
and now can be eaten by Jew and Gentile alike—without the slightest experience of indigestion. It is surprising that the hamantash has
not become the symbol of the National Conference of Christians
and Jews.

But we have hardly begun to scratch the surface of the hamantash. In its shape, the hamantash recalls the Napoleonic hat and thus
suggests the spirit of the conqueror. By contrast, the flattened latke
suggests the spirit of defeat, of surrender, of humiliation. In its taste
and its alimentary influence, the hamantash is purgative and cleansing. Can the same be said for the latke, which fills one up, symbolic
of the burdens and the weariness that Jewish flesh and spirit have
been heir to? But even more important is its name: the hamantash
keeps alive the eternal archetypal villain of Jewish history—Haman
rasha, the devil incarnate, the Jew persecutor. When we eat the
hamantash, we devour our enemy, convert him into excrement, celebrate our triumphs. When we eat a latke, is it possible to think of
triumph? The hamantash is the symbol of victory, the latke of defeat.

What can the defenders of the latke possibly say in return? They might argue perversely: that the latke is circular and the hamantash triangular, and isn't the circle the perfect geometric form? This would be a wistful ignoring of the fact that the hamantash, whatever its limitations, is one half of the Magen David, and that two hamantashen make a whole Magen David. They might say that the Christian suggestion in the hamantash undermines its kosher integrity, the brotherhood theme notwithstanding. And they might also deny the pleasure of eating Haman symbolically or otherwise. And finally against the claim that the latke in its flattened condition and its culinary heaviness suggests humiliation and defeat, they might counter with an exhortation against the sin of pride; they might insist that it is only proper to accept the burdens of life, and in what better way than by eating latkes. To this the hamantashnik can only reply with the authority of Bruno Bettelheim, that this is a most pernicious form of ghetto thinking.

Which leads to the whole question of the moral crisis in America. The hamantash, with its synthesizing ambition, with its militancy, optimism, cheerfulness, and sweet reasonableness, represents all that is desirable. It is on the side of decency without being square. What more is there to say but that the latke, with its hip tendencies, its radical hatred for all that is decent and wholesome and greaseless, must be eradicated from our way of life.

Noshes

In ancient Hebrew, letters were used to denote numbers as well as words. *Aleph* denoted 1, *bet* denoted 2, etc. Thus every word also denoted a number, and you could evaluate words. From this came numerology, the study of words and their related numbers. For English, let A = 1, B = 2, C = 3, etc., all the way to Z = 26. Adding up the values of the letters in hamantash, we get H = 8, A = 1, M = 13, etc., for a total of 88 or 85, depending upon whether you use a C (hamantasch) or not, or 92 or 89, depending upon whether you begin with H-A-M-A-N or H-A-M-E-N. These are not particularly significant numbers. But, if you apply this procedure to the word "latke," you get L = 12, A = 1, T = 20, K = 11, and E = 5, for a total of 49. An odd square. What more could one want? Any food whose letters add up to an odd perfect square must be perfect itself. ZALMAN USISKIN, *An Irreverent Symposiast*

✡   ✡   ✡

There is a basic opposition between the raw and the cooked; L-S has furthered this opposition to construct a culinary triangle, made up of the raw, cooked, and the rotten. The raw constitutes an unmarked pole, whereas the cooked and the rotten are strongly marked: the cooked is a cultural transformation of the raw, and the rotten its natural transformation. Thus, the combination of potato pancake that is fried and the accompanying dab of sour cream represents, in itself, both kinds of transformation.

It is well to end by recalling Lévi-Strauss's great reconstruction of the meaning of the latke: "The latke is selected not only because it is good to think but because it is good to eat." HARRY HAROOTUN-IAN, *Latkes and the Origins of Civilization*

✡   ✡   ✡

Note that hamantashen are never fried in oil. We have here what linguists call an opposition between oily and non-oily. What is the function of this opposition? Why is an oily Hanukkah opposed to a non-oily Purim? The reason is that the Purim story takes place in Persia and the Hanukkah story in Eretz Yisrael. Persia is associated with more than enough oil, and Israel . . . not enough. Each latke we eat represents our fervent prayer that the land that flows with milk and honey should, please G-d, also flow with petroleum. HOWARD ARONSON, *On the Symbolism of Latkes and Hamantashen*

✡   ✡   ✡

Let us first look at the most abstract symbolic level of the latke and hamantash. They are, of course, a circle and a triangle, which are the standard symbols in genealogical charts that anthropologists delight in drawing. The hamantash represents the triangle, the symbol for the male, and the latke the circle, the symbol for the female, which brings us in the best Lévi-Straussian analysis to binary opposition. In this conceptualization, the whole world is made up of opposing forces, ideas, and actions which all people represent in their myth and ritual, and well as in their social structure: yin and yang, up and down, hot and cold, light and dark, pure and impure, male and female, the latke and the hamantash. BERNARD S. COHN, *The Latke and the Hamantash: An Interactional Symbolic Analysis; or, "You Are What You Eat"*

✡   ✡   ✡

I proceed from the assumption that latkes and hamantashen are interesting because they stand for something else. I justify that assumption very simply: has anyone ever had a symposium on *kishke* and *knishes*? Have you ever heard of organized intellectual effort devoted to *knaydlekh* and *kreplakh*? Or a symposium on soup—borsht vs. *schav*? Thus I think it is safe to say that the latke and the hamantash force themselves on our attention because they stand for—or represent—something else. As we say in our circles, they have semiotic value. Our first task, then, is to discover what these significant objects stand for.

Claude Lévi-Strauss (descendant of rabbis of Versailles, as his impenetrable Talmudic writing clearly indicates) said that it was not the totemic objects that represent, but rather the significant difference between each contrasted pair. What, then, distinguishes a latke from a hamantash? Latkes are fried, whereas hamantashen are baked. This is a significant difference, which directs our attention to what Lévi-Strauss called *le triangle culinaire*, another strange bit of Yiddish, and not a very obscure reference to the hamantash. Lévi-Strauss's method directs us to discover the significant difference between these objects by finding what mediates between them. Between frying and baking, what do we have? Why boiling, quite obviously! Thus, we can say that chicken soup is the concrete representation of the significant opposition between the latke and the hamantash. RALPH W. NICHOLAS, *The Semiotic Value of Latkes and Hamantashen*

Round Seven

Shrouded in Mystery:
Spinning Latkes and Neutrinos

From Cain to Quincy:
Jewish Foods as Weapons of Violence

ROBERT KIRSCHNER

Through the years, many scholars have spoken to the great issue that faces us tonight. I believe, however, that I am the first forensic pathologist to lecture at this forum, and I will directly address the issue of Jewish foods as instruments of violence.

As I scanned the forensic literature, it was apparent that despite the wide range of violent deaths that are encountered by forensic pathologists around the world, there were no reports of serious injuries or deaths associated with either latkes or hamantashen. The *Vital Statistics of the United States* give no clue of the morbid significance of these foods, and there is no mention of either latkes or hamantashen in the *Weekly Morbidity and Mortality Report* published by the Centers for Disease Control. My first inclination was to suspect a conspiracy of silence. Was this an anti-Semitic effort, contrived to deny the latke and hamantash their rightful place in the history of murder and mayhem, or was this a Zionist conspiracy, designed to keep the gentile world unaware of the gastronomic masochism occasionally practiced by members of the Jewish faith? I finally came to the conclusion that there has simply been a failure to recognize the sometimes subtle evidence of latke or hamantash-induced injury, particularly since such injuries usually tend to be of an internal nature.

Tonight, of course, we only have time to scratch the surface of Judeo-gastronomic pathology. Those of you who watch Quincy on television know that the applications of forensic science do not limit themselves only to the violent and morbid aspects of today's world. The forensic pathologist uses all of the methods of modern science, often in pursuit of great truths that have little relevance to the profession, but result in higher Nielson ratings. That this is the case, we will demonstrate tonight.

Scripture tells us Cain slew Abel—a sign of a certain lack of brotherly affection that we still see upon occasion today. The Bible does not tell us by what means, but to a forensic pathologist, that evidence is essential. If we are to understand death and violence we must study the weapons involved. My search of illustrated biblical tales shows that most do not depict the world's first homicide. Illustrations that do exist are drawn for children or present a scenario of the assailant, his victim, and an anthropomorphic Jehovah passing judgment upon Cain. Certainly, God knows what took place, but what about the rest of us? Unfortunately, there was no forensic pathologist at the scene to examine the victim, to describe his injuries, or to give any clue as to the weapon that may have been used. However, my perusal of various sacred and profane texts has led me to the conclusion that the weapon employed was a hamantash, although it was not called by such a name until many centuries later. What is the evidence for this opinion?

Adam and Eve were forced to vacate the Garden of Eden on rather short notice. When they had left the garden, God's sense of humor revealed itself as Eve discovered that all she had with her were dried-out plums and some moldy wheat. Eve prepared dough from the wheat and, not knowing what else to do with the prunes, stuffed them into the dough, formed them into a shape that could easily be held in the hand, and baked them. While eating some of these archetypal hamantashen it must have occurred to Cain that they would better serve as weapons than as a source of sustenance. Cain crept up behind Abel, raised his hand holding the hamantash, and as Abel turned to greet his brother, brought the hamantash down upon his brother's head. An examination of this weapon shows the damage that might be inflicted not only by the hard, blunt edges but by the sharp points present at the corners of this alleged food product.

Let us turn now to a contemporary problem. Several months ago residents of Hyde Park noticed strange events at a house on Woodlawn Avenue. A shallow grave had been discovered in the basement and the contents were dug up and removed. Shortly thereafter residents of the house complained of strange vibrations and a few of the most pious claimed to see the fleeting image of a giant hamantash within the walls of the house. What had been removed from the grave was an ancient white cloth bearing Hebrew letters upon it. The letters formed the word "Shabbat," a seemingly inappropriate inscription for a burial cloth. The name of the artist is also inscribed. More interesting, however, was the fact that some claimed they saw in this cloth a faint gray triangular image. Others claimed that the cloth showed an almost three-dimensional pattern, the folds forming a triangular outline. Still others claimed to see in this cloth a distinct black triangular object having the appearance of a hamantash scorched by some supernatural process. It soon became clear that what had been discovered in the basement of the Hillel House was the long lost Shroud of Purim.

How this shroud came to rest within the confines of the University of Chicago campus we do not know. I suspect that it was spirited away from the Holy Land by an overzealous rabbi of an earlier generation. There are two questions regarding the shroud that we must answer. First, is this the original Shroud of Purim? And second, what were its contents?

As you know, when King Ahasuerus was informed of Haman's evil ways, he sent out orders that the Jews should take up weapons and prepare to defend themselves. The triangular pastry had many advantages as a weapon. It was small and could easily be concealed in the hand. It could be employed either as a blunt object or as a sharp, pointed instrument. The shape of the hamantash also gave remarkable aerodynamic stability when it was hurled through the air at its intended victim. And finally, if not put to use as a weapon, it could always be eaten.

Queen Esther probably spent little time in the kitchen. However, she followed the king's command and prepared a hamantash, wrapped it securely in her Shabbat *challeh* cloth, and stowed it away until needed. Haman, however, was quickly hanged. Esther had no need to call upon her secreted pastry, and it lay dormant within its covering for centuries.

We now have before us this shroud which some have claimed was used to wrap the original Purim hamantash. To determine whether it is the genuine article, we have subjected it to rigorous tests of modern forensic science and I shall present the evidence that we have gathered.

For our analysis we have used crumbs gently plucked from the shroud. The ghostly image of the hamantash that remains burned within the cloth suggests strongly that a supernatural force vaporized the hamantash without disturbing the original folds of the shroud. Electron microscopy reveals that the ultrastructure of these crumbs shows a biotic resemblance to cytoplasmic organelles.

The alleged hamantash granules are rather spherical and, in addition, show on their surface circular configurations which I believe are the evolutionary progenitors of the bagel. Using a Finnegan Computerized GC/Mass Spectrophotometer, we have programmed the essential raw data. Analysis of the material by mass chromatography shows a spectrum in which the prune, poppy seed, and wheat components are isolated. On the right-hand side of the spectrum we see only *schmutz* (dirt.) A typical modern-day latke spectrum is quite different. The potato spectrum is to the left, followed by the onion, and chicken *shmaltz* spectra. On the right side we see a typical rye bread spectrum. Analysis by mass spectrophotometry shows that the spectra of the crumbs from the shroud are those of a typical hamantash.

X-ray dispersive analysis reveals distinct peaks for both the filling and the shell. Another spectrum shows crumbs found on the floor of the Hillel House. Further analysis shows various components identified as the remains of a bagel and lox brunch. Carbon-14 dating was attempted, but was obscured by the large amount of carbon-12 that was present, the latter either the remnants of our supernatural vaporization process or possibly the result of Esther's failure to pay attention to the time that her hamantash was in the oven.

Scholars from all over the world have had access to the shroud and have examined it. Their reactions have ranged from exclamations of disbelief to exclamations of disgust. The kindest words have come from Rebbe Manischewitz of the yeshiva in New York. This Chasidic scholar stated forthrightly that the investigators in the project were all a little *meshugge*.

In conclusion, the debate over the authenticity of the Shroud of Purim continues. There is no doubt, however, of the rightful place of the hamantash as an instrument of violence in Jewish history.

A New Page in the History of Atomic Physics

JERROLD M. SADOCK

Many of us are probably familiar with Thomson's plum-pudding model of the atom. Thomson supposed that atoms consisted of a positively charged pudding loaded with insufficient negatively charged plums to neutralize the charge. I wonder, though, how many of us know of the contemporary Lapidus latke theory. According to Lapidus, matter was composed of myriad greasy little latkes each composed of equal amounts of positive bits of potato and negative bits of onion. These were not very good latkes, to be sure, but they were latkes nonetheless.

At sufficiently high temperatures, the small, oily cakes were free to slip and slide around each other, and anything kept at that temperature would assume the shape of the vessel which contained it. Here we have an elegant, if somewhat unappetizing, account of the liquid state of matter. Lowering the temperature would cause the grease to congeal, producing a solid. A little reflection on the recipe should convince us that Lapidus's latkes could easily account for gas as well.

Both the plum-pudding and latke models fell into disrepute, however, when the results of Rutherford's famous scattering experiments were made known. Rutherford showed that high-speed alpha particles would sometimes pass straight though thin gold foil as if nothing were there and would sometimes be scattered at varying angles. Neither culinary model seemed consistent with this result, and Thomson abandoned his theory.

Lapidus, on the other hand, was undaunted. Perhaps the latke had unknown properties which could account for Rutherford's data. He arranged to test his data in his small, ill-equipped laboratory and tailor shop. He fried huge batches of latkes and congealed them into sheets one latke thick. Alpha particles, which were thought to be quite massive for their size, he likened to his mother's *knaydlekh*. With a slingshot arrangement of his own design, Lapidus fired *knaydlekh* at various velocities at the latke sheets and observed the results. The principal result was to produce the most unsightly and least hygienic tailor shop in Eastern Europe, if not the world. Not a single *knaydl* ever passed straight though the latkes without making a *balagan*.

Despite his lack of experimental success, Lapidus continued to attack his opposition on theoretical grounds. In a little-read article entitled *"Farvoszhe a Hamantash,"* published in the first and only number of the Yiddish journal *Tsaytshrift far Purimdiker Fizik,* November 1912, he pointed out that Rutherford's nuclear model in which all of the heavy stuff was concentrated at the center of the atom—the hamantash model, as Lapidus termed it, was completely untested. I quote (my translation):

Has Rothenberg [sic] *ever cooked up a big bunch bunch hamantashen and thrown at it a piece filling? Does Rothenberg know how to make hamantashen yet? No and no!*

Realizing the difficulties with the latke theory, Lapidus produced and tested, in quick succession, the *lokshen kugel* theory, the *farfel* theory, the *kashe* theory, and finally the prune and carrot *tsimmis* theory. Again and again his consistently negative but very messy findings were ignored. He enlarged the scale of his experiments, but nobody paid any attention to him no matter how big a mess he made.

In 1914 he returned to his latke theory and made two advances which clearly anticipated the quantum mechanics of a decade and a half later. In trying to understand the nature of the latke itself, he realized in a flash that "latke" meant a little *lat*. But here was a fundamentally counterintuitive result. How could a *lat* be a little? "How can a particle be a wave?" we would put it nowadays.

Also in 1914, shortly after he received his conscription papers, an accident befell Lapidus which very nearly cost him a toe. Somehow, a gun that was very carefully aimed at one of his toes went off! Lapidus counted his toes and discovered to his horror that they were all there! In a burst of mathematical inspiration, he counted his toes twice and divided by two. Same answer. All there. He lifted his foot and there, in the inch-thick accretion of dried food that formed the floor of his tailor shop, right under the toe at which the gun had been aimed, was a bullet hole. Suddenly it dawned on him. His toes had moved and were not where he had thought they were. Latkes, he reasoned, were just like toes; well, pretty similar anyway. You just can't trust them to stay in one place too long. This he termed his *Ver Veys*, or uncertainty principle. Aside from a few pretty soiled gabardines, this was Lapidus's proudest achievement.

During the war, the physics business went downhill rapidly and the tailor business was only so-so. Lapidus moved to America and dropped out of sight. Rumor has it, though, that there's a little old man who lives in Miami Beach and who smiles each Purim when he sees hamantashen. He chuckles at the thought that he's the only one who realizes that hamantashen are composed of lots of little latkes.

The Scientific Method and the
Latke-Hamantash Issue

EDWARD W. KOLB

Rabbi Leifer was kind enough to allow free access to the archives
of Hillel, and I was able to research past Latke-Hamantash symposia. I was curious as to why, after forty-six years of consideration
and debate among members of our distinguished faculty, such a crucial issue had not been settled. What I discovered, to my utter amazement, is that this debate has been largely dominated by faculty from
the social sciences and humanities. Now anyone who has been
through a faculty meeting with these people knows quite well that
they never settle a damn thing, because deep down inside they just
love to argue. That is why the only real difference between a faculty
meeting and a preschool class is that the preschool class is run under
responsible adult supervision.

So, perhaps now it is time to settle, once and for all, the latke-
hamantash question by putting it to the rigorous, objective test of
the scientific method. What I will present to you now is not the
empty polemic of philosophers, social scientists, and humanists, but
rather the crystal-clear logic of science. I am afraid that many in the
audience might be intimidated by science, so to make it easier for
those of you who are used to the fuzzy, hazy, imprecise language of
the social sciences, I will start with a brief guide to the precise language of scientists to be found in the extensive Latke-Hamantash literature. For instance,

When it says:

"The hamantashen were integrated into the ambient background
environment,"

it really means:

"The hamantashen were dropped on the floor."
When it says:
"The latkes were kept isolated from adverse contaminants,"
it really means:
"The latkes were not dropped on the floor."
When it says:
"Three sample hamantashen were chosen for further analysis,"
it really means:
"Results of the others didn't make sense, so I omitted them from the analysis."
When it says:
"It is widely known that . . ."
it really means:
"I haven't bothered to look up the original reference, but . . ."
When it says:
"The final resolution awaits further experimental data,"
it really means:
"The experiments didn't work, but I need the publication for a grant."
When it says:
"I would like to thank Winstein for technical assistance and Friedman for valuable discussions,"
it really means:
"Winstein did the experiment and Friedman told me what it meant."

You see, science is not so difficult. Now that you are all comfortable with the precise language of science, let us proceed. The first step is to research the scientific literature on the subject. The latke-hamantash question has been the subject of scientific inquiry ever since the birth of modern science.

Perhaps the first modern physics experiment involved latkes and hamantashen. In 1590, the father of modern science, Galileo Galilei, then an associate professor at the University of Pisa, was having breakfast, al fresco, at the Pizzeria atop the Leaning Tower of Pisa. It was quite windy that morning, and a strong gust happened to cause a waiter to drop a tray of food off the top of the tower. Galileo was amazed to see that a latke and a hamantash the waiter dropped hit the ground at precisely the same instant. This led Galileo to postulate the first law of mechanics, which states, "A pound of latkes weighs the same as a pound of hamantashen." This overturned Aristotle's claim that latkes fall faster than hamantashen. This law can be found in Galileo's immortal book, *Il diagolo sopra i due massimi sistemi del cibo, latke e hamantash* or *The Dialogue Concerning the Two Great Food Systems, Latke and Hamantash.* It is, of course, because of this work that Galileo later faced the Inquisition, because experimentation with kosher food was considered heresy by the Church in the sixteenth century. Galileo later repeated his pioneering experiment. Of course he could not bring himself to throw such tasty delicacies as latkes and hamantashen off the tower, so he tossed two of his graduate students off the tower and noted that they hit the ground at exactly the same time.

The belief that the physics of latkes and hamantashen is explained by the experiments of Galileo was overturned in the revolution of twentieth-century physics, led by that great latke/hamantash gourmet, Albert Einstein. Historians of science agree that Einstein was led to the special and general merits of the latke and the hamantash. As we shall see, Einstein's theories will play a large role in my own theory, the basis of which I will soon describe.

The next step is to sample some data. I started by sampling an entire plate of prune-filled hamantashen. I found them so tasty that I went through the entire plate of hamantashen in about five minutes. And in another five minutes, the entire plate of hamantashen had gone through me. After this experience I decided to stick to my own field of purely theoretical research, so now let me turn to my own theoretical path of study to resolve the latke/hamantash problem.

Consistent with modern theories of relativity and quantum field theory, the entire latke/hamantash question can be decided only by studying their basic constituents. Now by "basic constituents" I am not talking about the ingredients given in cookbooks. That is stupid, boring chemistry. Rather, I refer to the most fundamental building blocks of the food itself, its quark structure. It is the quark structure of the latke and hamantash that contains all the relative information about their structure, and any attempt to judge the relative merits of the two without a complete understanding of their quark structure is doomed to failure, and will degenerate into the mere philosophical discussion we wish to avoid. Sadly, the quark structure of latkes and hamantashen has received precious little attention from scientists. This is due, no doubt, to the scandalous state of the National Science Foundation and the Department of Energy budgets. What I will unveil now is the outline for a sound scientific program to study the latke/hamantash quark structure. This program is courageous in scope, bold in vision, and, I am most proud to say, damned expensive.

The traditional method of exploring the quark structure of matter is through colliding things together at enormous energies. This is usually done by means of an accelerator, such as the 4.26-mile circumference Tevatron ring at Fermi National Accelerator Laboratory, thirty miles northwest of here in Batavia, Illinois. Unfortunately, the Fermilab Tevatron accelerator, as large as it is, is simply not powerful enough to handle the extreme energies necessary for latke/hamantash collisions. Many of you are familiar with the superconducting supercollider, or SSC, the 56-mile-long accelerator now under construction in Waxahachie, Texas. This seven-billion-dollar boondoggle, excuse me, accelerator, might be powerful enough, but unfortunately it has been rendered *traife* by the acceleration of Texas tacos.

Clearly, what is needed is a separate accelerator, designed for, and dedicated to, latke/hamantash research. I am happy to report to you this evening that physicists at the University of Chicago, technicians at the Argonne National Laboratory, and scientists at Fermilab have come up with a design for a machine powerful enough to accelerate either latkes or hamantashen to sufficient energies to unlock the secrets of their quark structure.

This new machine, the Superconducting Super Hamalatkatron, or SSH for short, can be constructed at the modest cost of 8.264 billion dollars, a price which includes tax, tip, and dealer prep. Also included is a factory rebate program for first-time accelerator owners that includes free rustproofing and pinstripes. The machine would stretch from Hyde Park on the eastern end, to Argonne at the southwestern end, out to Fermilab on the western front. Latkes would be injected into the accelerator at a location convenient to Morry's Deli, while hamantash would be injected at the Argonne Laboratory. The food would be accelerated to high energy using the single strongest force known, the force of guilt. The latkes and hamantashen would then collide, spewing their basic ingredients through the air. Hidden in the debris of the collision will be clues to the quark structure of the latke and hamantash.

Everyone knows that knowledge does not come cheaply. The tremendous cost of this machine would be shared by the University of Chicago, the City of Chicago, and the DOE (Department of Ethnicity). To raise its share of the cost of the SSH, the university will have to tighten its belt a bit. We have proposed that this be accomplished by closing a few departments, such as Philosophy, Slavic Languages, the Divinity School, and the Departments of Near Eastern Languages, Far Eastern Languages, Middle Eastern Languages, South Eastern Languages, and North by Northwest Eastern Languages.

How can we convince the federal government to pay for its share of the SSH? In this era of decreasing budgets for government-supported basic scientific research, it is no longer sufficient that the program answer fundamental questions such as the relative merits of latke versus hamantash. The government demands that scientific research have some immediate benefit to society, such as curing some terrible disease, or helping our economic competitiveness. This is where the technological spin-offs of the SSH are important.

The SSH will do much more than settle the latke/hamantash question. Once the quark structure of the latke and the hamantash are known, we will be able to exploit this knowledge to solve many of the most important problems facing society. Knowledge gained from the SSH will have a payoff all congressmen will be sure to appreciate, a cure for male pattern baldness! And what about our new female senators? Preliminary results published in the *New England Journal of Medicine* have shown that beams extracted from the SSH, directed to the thighs or buttocks, can dissolve cellulite in a quick, painless process. Yes, here we see yet another example of the benefits to society of basic research.

Finally, with a complete map of the quark structure of latkes and hamantashen we will have in hand the final piece of the puzzle for our complete understanding of the universe. We will have a picture starting with the primordial chicken soup in the early universe, through the era of production of nuclei, the era of production of atoms, the era of production of molecules, the era of the emergence of life on our planet, through the development of Jewish cooking, known to cosmologists as the era of cholesterol.

Although I cannot give you a definitive answer at this moment, we are very close. After one or two years of operation of the SSH, we should have the final answer to these fundamental questions. Finally, we can see that glorious day when the latke/hamantash issue is forever removed from the realm of philosophers and others trained in the humanities, and is placed firmly in the sphere of rational scientific inquiry. Thank you.

Paired Matter, Edible and Inedible

LEON M. LEDERMAN

Before we get too deeply into the debate of this evening I want to tell you a story. This has to do with the research that colleagues and I carried out in 1962 which resulted in the award of the Nobel Prize in Physics and very probably the reason why I am here tonight. It's hard to believe that because of some Swedish ladies and gentlemen years ago, I am engaged in the Hamantash-Latke Debate.

In 1962 we studied the curious properties of a subnuclear particle called the neutrino. Our experiment gave the astonishing result that there were in fact not one neutrino but *two* neutrinos. What we found was ultimately interpreted in the following way: it is not enough to describe an electron by itself; a complete description would add one of the neutrinos—the electron neutrino. Similarly it is not enough to describe a muon: one needs to add its neutrino. Ever since that time, in particle physics, the particles of matter must be *paired*. Aha! You begin to see a distant light!

Now such a pairing infiltrates into every corner of intellectual activity. I'll give you some examples. Let's take mathematics, where dichotomic variables are used to describe an essential pair, illustrated by a dyadic, a two-element column matrix which is related to the two base elements which describe everything in the field of two dimensions. The word "dichotomy" is derived from this and expresses the division into two parts, sharply distinguished or opposites. And so it is with latkes and hamantashen, distinguished by symmetry, by form, color, and induced hormonal and glandular reactions. Much of this was borrowed from the Hebrew prophet and philosopher Ezekiel, who wrote a popular hit song, "Di-aynnu."

Computer scientists have their "o" and "I," to which all cognition is reduced in the digitalization of human knowledge.

Political scientists used to have their proletariat and bourgeois antipodes, which have recently gone the way of distinctions between Democrat and Republican. However the very word "conservative" loses its meaning without the contrast to "liberal."

In economics can we have macro without micro? Friedman without Samuelson? Nevermind.

Proceeding to anthropology, we are immediately led to the great French social anthropologist Claude Lévi-Strauss. Now his structuralism seeks, like the physicists, an underlying simplicity (which he calls universality) in human culture. Thus he seeks for binary contrasts, opposites, in a search for the basic components out of which meaning is constructed. Nature and culture is a key binary system. This spills over to kinships like brother-sister, parent-child, etc.

By now my theme is clear: the total irrelevance of this evening's debate must be obvious. It makes no more sense to prefer latkes to hamantashen or hamantashen to latkes than to extol hot over cold, the chicken over the egg, the male over the female, the savory over the sweet, the clan over the network.

One can no more live with only latkes than one can live with only north, or only an up quark, or only lox . . .

To have latkes without hamantashen is like having the *VAY* without the *OI!*

The fundamental complementarity of the hamantash with its corners and a properly made latke with its absence of corners is precisely the complementarity of particles and waves, energy and time, Simon and Schuster, *Litvaks* and *Galitzianers*, positives and negatives, the yin and the yang, scotch and soda, the hard and the soft, the good and the evil . . .

You can no more live with H alone or L alone than you can take home your favorite end of a piece of string, leaving the other end to fend for itself in an unfriendly world. Neither can you separate and take home the north pole of a bar magnet or only one pistachio nut.

Thus, my friends, the debate is devoid of logical structure, illogical structure, or even mythological structure.

Noshes

I have been asked by Apple Computer to use this august occasion to unveil to you tonight the newest member in the Macintosh family of computers. This, Ladies and Gentlemen, is the New Generation of Macintoshen, Son of Macintosh, Ben Macintosh Hamantash. Looks like a real hamantash, doesn't it? Well, you all have heard of prune hamantashen, cherry hamantashen, lemon hamantashen, poppy-seed hamantashen. This is an Apple Hamantash.

Now, you have all seen disposable cameras; the Apple Hamantash is the first edible computer. When you run out of memory, you just eat your computer. To prove to you that this is no joke, I'm going to take a bite out of this, in fact, I'm going to take a megabyte. Here goes. JOSEF STERN, *Thesis, Antithesis, Blintzes*

✡ ✡ ✡

Let me dwell for a moment on the latke as inspiration in scientific research. Columbus discovered America in 1492. The potato was brought back to Europe. Almost immediately the potato displaced grain as the basic ingredient in latkes. One can trace the diffusion of the modern latke throughout Europe followed shortly afterward by extraordinary bursts of creative energy.

Renaissance, yes, but of the latke. How else was Kepler able to arrive at the ellipsoidal shape of the orbits of the planets around the sun but by contemplation of the appearance of the well-cooked latke? How else to account for the decrease of the vigor of Italian science in the late Renaissance but by the displacement of the latke by pasta and its subsequent degeneration to mere gnocchi? Can one believe that the fall of an apple is sufficiently inspiring to lead Newton to the theory of universal gravitation? But the slither of a latke to the floor as one attempts to cut it: that is thought-provoking in the extreme. Would that Newton could have admitted the truth.

MORREL H. COHEN, *Latkes, Hamantashen, and the History of Science*

☆　　☆　　☆

"Which Is Better: The Latke or Hamantash?" is not a valid question, even though this has been debated now for fifty years.

- *The question does not exhibit the necessary property of universality.*
- *It is culturally biased, implies gender specificity, exhibits geographical chauvinism and appeals to special interests.*
- *It is not value-free.*

This question would not pass scrutiny on an SAT test, since it unfairly favors one ethnic and gender group over another: e.g., it favors the NY and Brooklyn establishment over the Midwest Rust Belt, and pits female latke workers against male hamantash bakers. In short, it is Politically Incorrect. Physics does not ask which is better: the proton or neutron, baryon or lepton, helium or neon, the conductor or insulator. These are simply properties of nature. Rather, physics asks: "Why?" or "Which is more important or more fundamental?" or "Who published it first? ISAAC ABELLA, *Grand Unification Theory: The Latke/Hamantash Paradigm in Postmodern Physics*

Round Eight

Appealing to
a Higher Authority

The Rights and Wrongs of Latkes

GEOFFREY R. STONE

It is my thesis, which I shall demonstrate with all the rigor of legal reasoning, that the latke has historically been the principal driving force behind the constitutional protection of free speech in the United States, whereas the hamantash has been a powerful force for censorship. Put simply, the latke is the Judah Maccabee of constitutional law; the hamantash, the Haman.

Consider, first, *Abrams v. United States*. During World War I, the United States sent a contingent of marines to Vladivostok. The defendants in *Abrams*, a group of Russian-Jewish immigrants who were self-proclaimed socialists and anarchists, perceived the expedition as an attempt by the United States to crush the Russian revolution. In protest, they threw several thousand copies of each of two leaflets, one in English, the other in Yiddish, from a rooftop in the Lower East Side of New York. The leaflets called for a general strike.

The defendants were promptly arrested by the military police. After a circus-like trial, the defendants were convicted of conspiring to obstruct the war effort. The trial judge sentenced each of them to twenty years in prison.

The defendants appealed to the Supreme Court, claiming that the convictions violated their rights under the First Amendment. The Court disagreed. What is memorable about *Abrams*, however, is not the Court's decision, but the dissenting opinion of that great Chasidic scholar, Oliver Wendell Holmes, for it was in Holmes's dissenting opinion that our constitutional protection of free speech first found full articulation. Holmes wrote:

Persecution for the expression of opinion seems to me perfectly logical. . . . But when men have realized that time has upset many fighting faiths, they may come to believe even more than they believe the very foundations of their own conduct that the ultimate good desired is better reached by free trade in ideas— that the best test of truth is the power of the thought to get itself accepted in the competition of the market. That, at any rate, is the theory of our Constitution.

Now, you ask, what has *this* to do with latkes? I will tell you. But first, it is essential to understand that what Holmes *really* objected to in *Abrams* was not so much the fact of conviction itself, but the severity of the punishment. As he explained, and I quote:

In this case, sentences of twenty years imprisonment have been imposed for the publishing of two leaflets. . . . Even if I am . . . wrong [in concluding that no crime has been committed, it seems to me that] the most nominal punishment [is] all that possibly could be inflicted, unless the defendants are to be made to suffer, not for their pathetic attempt to call a strike, but for the creed they avow, a creed that no one has a right to consider.

Thus, what inspired Holmes's dissent in *Abrams* was his *suspicion* that the defendants were being punished not for attempting to obstruct the war, but for the *offensiveness* of their ideas. How did he know this? Listen to the statement of the *trial* judge, just before sentencing the defendants. Again, I quote:

These defendants took the stand. They talked about capitalists and producers, and I tried to figure out what a capitalist and what a producer is as contemplated by them. After listening carefully to all they had to say, I came to the conclusion that a capitalist is a man with a decent set of clothes, a minimum of $1.25 in his pocket, and a good character. And when I tried to find out what the prisoners had produced, I was unable to find out anything at all. So far as I can learn, not one of them ever produced so much as a single . . . potato.

And there it is: a single *potato*! And what sort of potato are we speaking of here? Remember these were Russian-Jewish émigrés. Why would *they* raise a potato? To make vichyssoise? To makes potatoes au gratin? Ridiculous. The *only* reason they would raise a potato is to make . . . latkes! But if, as the trial judge declared, they "did not raise even a single potato," what does *this* tell us? It tells us that the defendants did not *like* latkes! And it was this that offended the trial judge; it was this "creed" of the defendants that led to the severity of their punishment; and it was thus latkes that ultimately led Holmes to write his eloquent defense of free speech, known ever since as the "marketplace of potatoes" theory of the First Amendment.

Now, as a blue-blood Chasidic scholar, Holmes was, of course, a committed devotee of the latke. Keeping in mind the defendants' creed of antilatkeism, it is thus understandable that during the course of his dissenting opinion Holmes described the defendants as "puny anonymities" and condemned their "creed" as "the creed of ignorance and immaturity." Indeed, at one point Holmes went so far as to attack the defendants' antilatkeism as, and I quote, a creed "we loathe and believe to be fraught with death." It is noteworthy that Holmes's deep personal contempt for the defendants' disdain for latkes makes even more impressive his willingness to protect their advocacy of their creed.

But the role of the latke in *Abrams* runs even deeper. For only one justice joined Justice Holmes's dissenting opinion—the first Jewish justice, Louis Brandeis. Brandeis, or course, earned his reputation before being appointed to the Court by fighting the infamous hamantashen trust in Boston. It was Brandeis who single-handedly crushed this cartel, which had conspired to corner, indeed, to tricorner, the hamantashen market. It was through this triumph, of course, that Brandeis earned his lifelong nickname, "Louis the Latke" Brandeis.

I would like now to move to another great decision in the evolution of our free speech tradition: *New York Times v. United States*—the Pentagon Papers Case.

In June of 1971, a former Pentagon official, Daniel Ellsberg—like Abrams, another socially conscious Jewish kid—gave the *New York Times* and the *Washington Post* a top secret Defense Department study. Upon learning of this leak, the United States immediately sought to enjoin the *Times* and the *Post* from publishing this material. The government claimed that such publication would interfere with the national security, lead to the death of soldiers, undermine our alliances, and prolong the war in Vietnam.

Within days the case worked itself to the Supreme Court, which held that the First Amendment prohibits any prior restraint. As Justice Black explained, "In the First Amendment, the Framers gave the free press the protection it must have to fulfill its essential role in our democracy. The press was to serve the governed, not the governors."

Think how far the Court had come from 1917, when the defendants in *Abrams* received twenty-year sentences for distributing their "puny" leaflets, to 1971, when two major newspapers were held to have a constitutional right to publish excerpts from a stolen top secret report in the face of government claims that publication would seriously jeopardize the national interest.

What explains this extraordinary transformation? Latkes, of course! To understand this phenomenon, it is essential to note that the critical precedent for the Court's highly speech-protective decision in the Pentagon Papers Case was its decision forty years earlier in *Near v. Minnesota*.

In *Near*, a state court issued an injunction prohibiting any further publication of a weekly magazine, the *Saturday Press*, because it had run a series of articles falsely asserting "that a Jewish gangster was in control of bootlegging in Minneapolis." In reversing this state court injunction, the Supreme Court held that such "prior restraints" on expression are unconstitutional. It was this principle, first stated in 1931 in *Near*, that provided the foundation for the Pentagon Papers decision some forty years later.

But note: the allegation that led to the litigation in *Near* was that the *Saturday Press* had falsely reported that a Jewish gangster was in control of bootlegging in Minneapolis. Now, I ask you: what does one use to make bootleg liquor? Potatoes, of course. But we know that the *Saturday Press*'s charge was false. So, the alleged gangster was not making illegal liquor. What, then, was he doing with all those potatoes?

The answer, of course, is clear—what would a Jew engaged in some form of manufacturing be doing with truckloads of potatoes? Making latkes, of course! And so it was that a humble latke manufacturer in Minnesota in 1931 managed to bring about the Pentagon Paper decision in 1971, which in turn led to the break-in of Daniel Ellsberg's psychiatrist's office, which in turn led to the discovery of the White House plumbers, which in turn led to Watergate, which in turn led to the resignation of Richard Nixon. The lowly latke—marching through time!

The third decision I would like to call to your attention is *New York Times v. Sullivan*, which arose out of the civil rights movements in the South. L. B. Sullivan, the sheriff of Montgomery, Alabama, widely known as the "town of a thousand hamantashen," brought a libel action against four black clergymen and the *New York Times*. L. B. claimed that he'd been libeled by an advertisement that had been published by the clergymen in the *Times*.

Sullivan claimed that several statements in the advertisement were false. Specifically, he objected to the following passage, and I quote: "In Montgomery, Alabama, after students sang, 'My Country, 'Tis of Thee' on the State Capitol steps, their leaders were expelled from school, and truckloads of police armed with shotguns and tear-gas ringed the Alabama State College campus. When the entire student body protested to state authorities by refusing to re-register, their dining hall was padlocked in an attempt to starve them into submission."

L. B. claimed that this was false in three respects: First, the students had sung not "My Country, 'Tis of Thee," but the National Anthem. Second, the students had been expelled not for leading a demonstration at the Capitol, but for demanding service at a segregated lunch counter. And third, not the entire student body, but only most of it, had protested the expulsion.

Now, one might think that these errors border on the trivial, but an *Alabama* jury—containing not a single Jew—found in favor of L. B. Happily, the Supreme Court reversed. Noting that "we consider this case against the background of a profound national commitment to the principle that debate on public issues should be uninhibited, robust, and wide-open," the Court held the damage award unconstitutional and sent L. B. packing.

And so, you ask, what does *this* have to do with our symposium? Well, remember that a key issue in the dispute concerned the allegation that the expelled students had demanded service at "a segregated lunch counter." This was at a time when such segregation was rampant in the South. I want you to close your eyes for a moment and imagine the scene. It is a hot summer day in Montgomery. Nine black students defiantly seat themselves at the segregated lunch counter. They place their orders. The proprietor glares at them with hatred in his eyes. He points to the sign over the counter. It

reads: "We do not serve ... latkes. Hamantashen only." Oh, sure—
they claimed it was separate, but equal. They *said* the students could
get latkes down the street. But in the "town of a thousand hamantashen," separate was *not* equal.

And consider the other allegation that was central to the case—the
statement that truckloads of police ringed the campus when the student's "dining hall was padlocked in an attempt to starve them into
submission."

Let me read you a full account of the incident, published the next
day in the *Montgomery Daily Dreidel*. I quote: "It was brutally hot on
the campus of Alabama State College. Dust, tinged with the sweet
aroma of tear gas, swirled in the air, as more than a hundred of
Montgomery's finest munched hamantashen while standing guard
over campus property. The college had justly locked its Negro students out of the dining hall, and the students were hopping mad.
At one point, a mob of Negro troublemakers crowded by the padlocked dining hall door and chanted: "Aleph, bet, gimmel, dalid; our
faith in law is solid. Give us bagels, give us lox; give us latkes by the
box. We are starving, we need noshin'; keep your lousy hamantashen."

I rest my case. It all comes down to what the great legal realists
of the early years of this century first recognized. If you want to understand the law, you need not look to principles of precedents, poli-
cies, or prescriptions. You don't even have to know Latin. All you
really have to know is what the judge ate before assuming the
bench. And where the First Amendment is concerned, the lesson is
clear ... the proof is in the pancake.

The Bioethical Implications of the Latke-Hamantash Debate; or, Small Fry, Deep Fry, in Your Eye, Northrop Frye

JOHN D. LANTOS

The general decline in moral virtue over the centuries has implications for our topic today, the relative merits of latkes and hamantashen. If we could understand the roots of moral excellence or the causes of moral decline, we might be able to determine whether, and in what sense, latkes or hamantashen could be considered more or less virtuous.

Of course, this exercise is fraught with methodologic peril, as are all exercises in moral philosophy, because, as Alasdair McIntyre has pointed out, one of the problems with moral disclosure in the twentieth century is we don't agree about what the words mean. Take the word "philosophy." An anecdote can best illustrate what I mean by that word.

A young man was about to go out on his first date. Worried, he asked his father, "Dad, what if I can't think of anything to talk about?"

"Don't worry, son," his father replied. "If the conversation lags, you can always start a conversation by remembering the three Fs— food, family, and philosophy."

Sure enough, as the young man and his date sat eating dinner in a romantic restaurant, the conversation lagged. Remembering his father's advice, the young man asked about food. "Do you like latkes?" he asked.

"No," his date replied.

Another long silence ensued. Remembering, again, his dad's recommendations, he asked, "Do you have any brothers?"

"No," came the quick answer.

He was starting to sweat. He didn't know what to say. He racked his brain and finally thought of a philosophic question.

"Well, if you had a brother, would he like latkes?"

If you had a brother, would he like latkes? Or, we might ask, hamantashen, and which would he prefer? This, I believe, is the fundamental question before us. It is not whether latkes or hamantashen are, in some intrinsic, atemporal, and abstract way better or worse. As tempting as the Kantian approach might be—trying to determine what any rational latke would perceive as moral—our problem is, at the same time, both more human and more complex. If you had a brother, which would he prefer?

Thus, in my inquiry tonight, I will be hewing closer to Emmanuel Levinas, trying to determine the implications of culinary preferences for face-to-face human relationships and our notions of the good within a human community. Our relationships with different foodstuffs may be, as Buber pointed out, of the I-you type or the I-thou type. I will argue for a third type, overlooked by Buber, the I-tuber. Or, as Buber might have experienced if he had eaten latkes while exploring the coral reefs near Eilat, the I-scuber with Buber eating tubers. Of course, such a relationship could only be possible with a latke, not a hamantash, and the rest, I will demonstrate, is simply so much poppy filling.

In exploring the issues raised by the latke-hamantash antinomy, it is important to first determine what fundamental values are at stake. I take it as self-evident that the evaluation of any foodstuff will have an empiric and a rational component. We can ask which we actually prefer—latkes or hamantashen—and derive answers from public opinion surveys or some other social science *drek*—whims and fashions masquerading as truth or fact—and by such data we might be able to show, for example, correlations between culinary preferences and socioeconomic class, religiosity, early toilet-training experiences, or preferences for this or that sexual position. My concerns go deeper. The question is not which we prefer, but which we should prefer.

Even this, however, does not go far enough. Too often, I believe, concerns have focused on the moral values of the people who eat latkes and hamantashen, and not enough attention has been paid to the internal subjective experiences of the latkes and hamantashen themselves. If this is the case, and if we are now at a stage in Western moral thought where a fundamental transformation of values is crucial, it should be possible to begin looking at the debate from the perspective of the latkes and hamantashen, and use them to ground our understanding of the inherent moral, legal, and political rights of different foodstuffs. To ask the question a different way, "Do latkes and hamantashen have rights? Are they equal rights? And if not, which might be considered morally superior?"

I had initially planned to do surveys of latkes and hamantashen themselves, finding out how they feel, evaluating their quality of life and preferences for life-sustaining treatment, etc., but I could not get that study through our institutional review board.

But to ask whether food has rights is to immediately establish connections between latke-hamantash debates and many of the burning issues in bioethics over the last decades. "Is it morally preferable to kill your food or let it die?" "When does latkehood begin?" "Would it be morally acceptable to clone a hamantash?" Issues of race, gender, and ethnicity come up. Why do Idaho potatoes cost more? Does it have anything to do with color? Can we give growth hormone to hamantashen? But I wish to focus on issues of potato identity, or what I call tuberhood.

Imagine, if you will, that you are riding a trolley car which is speeding downhill on a straight line of track. The track goes through a narrow valley, with steep hills on both sides. On the track ahead of you are seven giant hamantashen. They see the trolley coming but cannot escape. If you hit the hamantashen, they will be immediately destroyed. Riding in the trolley with you is a large latke. Imagine further that there is a fork in the track, and that you can pull the switch at the back of your trolley, which will turn you onto a side spur or rail, saving the lives of the seven hamantashen. However, your path to the switch is blocked by the large latke. Now, here is the moral question: would it be acceptable to take positive action—that is—eating the latke, in order to save the hamantashen? Or, on the other hand, would it be morally preferable to do nothing, allowing the hamantashen to be run over simply by, as it were, letting nature take its course? Most of you, I'm sure, would be loathe to eat the latke in that situation, illustrating, I think, that latkes have rights, trolley cars have utility, and hamantashen are both relativistic and deontological.

I can point this out more pointedly by another, perhaps more relevant, example. The Talmud tells the story of Rabbi Bambam, who was hiking in the Swiss Alps one Purim with his uncle and five other hikers, including a three-hundred-pound man who was gorging himself on hamantashen throughout the trip. The uncle fell off a cliff and was critically injured. By the time Bambam reached him, he was close to death, but he whispered to Bambam that he had always hated his wife's hamantashen but could never tell her. Now that he was dying, however, he wanted the rabbi to promise that he would give all his money to a latke factory. The rabbi, with some misgivings, promised, in order to ease the passing of his dying uncle. The rabbi was wondering whether he was obligated.

On the way home, the hiking party stopped to rest in a small cave. When it came time to leave, the fat man went out first and got stuck in the mouth of the cave. They couldn't move him in or out. Furthermore, he kept stuffing himself with hamantashen, growing fatter and fatter. The men in the party asked the rabbi whether it would be permissible, even though it was Purim, to withhold the hamantashen, allowing the fat man to lose enough weight so that the rest of them could get out of the cave and their lives be saved.

The rabbi's answer was interesting. Imagine, he said that you went to sleep one night and woke up and you were connected, by an elaborate life-support system to a hamantash which was also a world class violinist. If you disconnected yourself from the hamantash, it would die. Wouldn't it be horrible, the rabbi asked, to go through life connected to a hamantash? To which his followers replied, "What does that have to do with the fat man?" To which the rabbi replied, "Do you think I should give the money to the latke factory?" To which his followers replied, "Why do you always answer a question with a question?" To which the rabbi replied, "Can't a question be an answer?" To which his followers replied, "Are you trying to avoid the question?" I can only add that it was a very good question.

Having thus convincingly shown that hamantashen do not have inherent moral rights, I would like to move the discussion off this anthropological level, and discuss some of the issues surrounding the latke. In particular, I think we need to establish the difference between the mere biological existence of a potato, or any other vegetable, and what I refer to as "tuberhood," that is, those moral qualities which distinguish a tuber existentially and teleologically from any other collection of complex carbohydrates. If tuberhood means anything at all, it means that there is a fundamental, existential, nonanthropomorphic, ahistorical, and transcendental value which all rational tubers share.

Here is a case to illustrate this: Two potatoes wanted to have children, but one had no eyes. A yam offered to donate an eye. A few years later, a little sweet potato needed a kidney transplant. The question was, how many eyes and how many nays would be sufficient to harvest the kidney, and wouldn't doing so treat the yam as a means, rather than an end in itself? Moral laws imply absolute necessity, not just for men but for all rational beings, be they human, flower, or tuber. So imagine, for a moment, that your best friend, a latke, was wanted by the police. While riding a trolley on her way to donate an eye, she noticed a policeman, and ran to hide in your basement. The police come to the door. They ask, "Have you seen any latkes?" Most reasonable people would be troubled, I would argue, telling the truth to the police under those circumstances, but most of us, I feel confident, would feel no qualms sharing a hamantash or two with an officer of the law, illustrating irrefutably, I believe, the unbreakable connection between latkes, Kant, and the Keystone Cops.

I believe that I have shown that one should eat the latke, turn the trolley car, tell the truth, donate kidneys, be loyal to our friends, and that these factors, as well as some previously unrecognized connections between Buber and the tuber clearly demonstrate the superior virtues of the latke over the hamantash. If you don't agree, I think you are stupid, and as Aristotle said, there is no point in discussing morality with stupid people.

Noshes

We have in law a great index of all legal materials in some one hundred volumes—the West American Digest System. Where do we find latke and hamantash in the law's digest tracts? The arresting answer is that we do not find them; we look in vain under the law's rubrics—*res gestae, res ipsa loquitur, coram nobis, quo warranto, quo vadis*. They are not indexed in the digest. From this I can only conclude that in the law's view the latke and the hamantash cannot be digested: they remain indigestible. HARRY KALVEN, JR., *Undigested Tensions in the Warren Supreme Court: Latke v. Hamantash; An Essay in Gastronomic Jurisprudence*

✡   ✡   ✡

Richard Wagner's tetralogy, *The Ring of the Nibelungen*, is constructed around a metaphor, a metaphor of good and evil, of the earthly and the underworld, of the powers of light and the redemption by love, and of the powers of darkness and the renunciation of love. The central image of evil, the ring itself, is of course merely a symbol whose significance can be readily discerned. A material found underground is loosed on the world; to use it one must renounce love. In doing so, he becomes capable of transforming the material into unique forms possessing the magical power of evil. It is clear that the material, the underworld gold, is but a metaphor for the potato. Alberich steals it from the three Rhinemaidens, renounces love, and is thereby capable of transforming the gold into two forms—the ring and the *Tarnhelm*. The ring, with all its powers for evil, is clearly a symbol for the latke itself . . .

With all this evil abroad on the earth, Wotan calls on the Walküre, and particularly Brunnhilde, to aid the gods. But Brunnhilde will not serve evil, and in punishment Wotan strips her of her godhood and puts her to sleep within a circle of fire. This latter cannot but bring to our consciousness the frying pan in which the latke must be prepared.

The three maidens, who represent, of course, the triangular hamantash, express their joy in the words "eia haheia!" Nonsense syllables on the surface, but onomatopoetically unmistakable as "hamantashen." PHILIP GOSSETT, *The Representation of Evil in Richard Wagner's Der Ring des Nibelungen*

Mythdefying Origins

Euripides' *The Cooks of Troy*, Hecuba's Lament

MARTHA C. NUSSBAUM

(Hecuba enters. She is a mess. Her clothing is spattered with all sorts of gooey and sticky foods, among which egg and peanut butter can be observed; sugar and jam have clearly been thrown around, and stick liberally to the peanut butter. Around her waist are strapped cooking implements, including a spatula, an eggbeater, a long-handled fork, and a large pie knife.)

> Up, unhappy head, up from the dust.
> This is no longer Troy.
> And I, Hecuba, was the chief cook of Troy.
> Now we are routed by the Greek onslaught
> that laid waste the gleaming kitchen of the kings,
> —Greeks greedily gorging on my cakes
> (both the round cakes and the sweet pointed cakes)
> with a gluttony that knew no moderation.
> Alas, the battle of the kitchen lost. Alas, my ruined royal
>   garments.
> Yield to fortune, yield to spilled dishwater.
> Don't hold life's prow against the swelling tide of garbage.

Aiai. (In an ancient ritual gesture, she beats her breast with a spatula.)

> What cause for grief is absent, when I have lost
> my ladles, my country, my husband, my Cuisinart?
> Oh, sweetest kitchen, heaped in the wintertime
> with those swelling rounded cakes

made from a root grown deep within the earth, sacred to Gaia?
And in springtime, oh, sweetest kitchen,
heaped with those extremely sweet pointed cakes,
shaped like the hat of a murderous Greek,
filled with the sweet fruit of the plum tree,
with added sugar, sacred to Dionysus.
Oh, pride of my ancestors! Oh, kitchen fragrant and warm,
all gone, all vanished, vanished in the morning,
just as turtle soup vanishes in the rosy light of dawn.

Oh, you Greek murderers:
Know well that those foods exist by nature,
not by our human conventions only.
My Trojan women, beware: an insolent assault
on truth and objectivity corrupts our cities.
The Think-Academies of Troy teem with corrupters of the
     young
who whisper that the rounded winter cake
is but a trick of human thought or fancy,
the pointed springtime cake, so full of plummy sugar,
a mere invention of our mortal minds.
Not so, I say: no mortal custom brought them to birth.
The unwritten and unfailing law of Zeus
commanded us to make and eat many of these cakes,
so delicious, and so nicely full of sugar.
By nature they exist, and by nature
they are good. Those who in their pride
deny this will surely know a barren kitchen:
Rancid milk, curdled custard,
soufflés fallen into a limp disgusting heap,
grey, tasteless, overcooked broccoli,
all these things the Olympian gods send to the cook
who claims that these cakes exist by convention, not by nature.

Still more full of wind the man
who claims that these cakes derive from an alien people,
a wild Asian tribe with strange festivals,
dwelling around the desert of Judaea.

No, no. These entirely delicious cakes
were born here, on the fertile plains of Troy.
The round cake is a child of this earth, sacred to Gaia.
A famine was upon us: the Trojan plain was barren.
Even brave warriors cried out from hunger,
when up from the ground shot lovely rounded cakes,
sizzling in oil,
sent by the hands of Gaia and Demeter.
At the sight of the cakes, a general cry went up,
and Calchas the seer, spoke in tones of prophecy:
"My children, the gods have sent these cakes
to save us from destruction, which in Greek we call *lusis*.
Therefore, let us call the cake *lutkes*, and teach this name
to our children in all future generations.
Sing sorrow, sorrow, but may dinner win out in the end."
So spoke the seer,
giving a name to the cakes that were born from nature.
And thus the name that he gave, *lutke*,
also exists by nature, not by convention.
Today there are some people who change the name,
calling the round cake "latke"—but they ignore
nature, and they will have a barren kitchen.

(She pauses to sample some of the jam and sugar that are sticking to her clothing.)

As for the pointed cake, filled with plummy sweetness,
this cake was brought to our city by the dancing god
Dionysus, lord of the vine's teeming clusters.
He made its shape to mock the hat of his enemy
the tyrant Pentheus, who once said to the god:
"Ha. Ha. I prefer men to
gods, and Dionysus is a piece of trash."
We therefore call this cake "ha-men-trash."
Once again, this name exists by nature, not by convention.
Those who say otherwise, or change the name in any way,
even by a single letter,
prove themselves desperate villains who would probably

do all manner of vile things against nature,
such as strange couplings, clonings of children,
and even bringing women into the sacred halls of science.

But why do I remain silent?
Destroyers of the cakes, hear my prediction.
For a vision is upon me. I see
the triumph of nature is at hand.
A time will come, in a distant land
beyond the edges of the wine-dark sea,
a land guarded by the monsters of the midway
eleven rather weak and useless Bears,
and the somewhat greater but somewhat unreliable
force of five once-great Bulls,
A time will come when the lofty halls of learning
set amid the groves of almond trees
will swell with the sweet speech of cakes,
and thousands will cheer the sizzling cake of Gaia
and thousands the sweet cake of Dionysus.
And I, Hecuba, restored to my office in the royal kitchen,
will find my Cuisinart, my ladles, my large supply of sugar,
and many will come to my biggest dinner party.

Until that day, I lean my body against the earth.
I hail my kitchen in its affliction,
with ancient gestures of grief,
beating my breast with spatula—*otototoi*,
tearing my hair with a fork, *aiai*.
Mourn for the ruined city, mourn for the *lutke* and the
     ha-men-trash,
then go find a small snack,
in the kitchens of the Greek ships.

The Secret History
of the Hamantash in China

JUDITH ZEITLIN

It is a great pleasure to be here tonight. How rarely in academic life
these days are we actually granted an occasion on which to act out
our deepest and most atavistic impulses: to indulge in arguments as
pompous, spurious, specious, and tasteless as we please!

Given the lamentable Eurocentric bias of the academy, I doubt
that many of you are aware that China is the only culture in the
world that can claim a three-thousand-year-old unbroken history
for the hamantash, beginning more than a millennium before the
Common Era, and continuing up through our own twentieth century. Now, a case could be made that the progenitors of *both* the
hamantash *and* the latke were invented by the ancient Chinese, but
given the enormity of the topic, and the difficulty and quantity of the
primary sources, I will limit the subject of my inquiry tonight to the
hamantash (arguably the more influential of the two forms anyway),
with only occasional forays into Chinese latke lore.

For convenience' sake, I will divide the long history of the
hamantash in China into a sequence of three major periods: the ancient phase, the early modern phase, and the semi-colonial, semi-imperialist phase. I hasten to add that I realize that these periodiza-
tions are certainly open to debate and that in so characterizing Chinese hamantash history I am forsaking traditional historiography's
preferred periodization by dynasty. I am convinced, however, that
these three phases are the key turning points in the development of
hamantashen in China and that none of my three phases can be reduced to a single dynasty.

In his introduction to that weighty tome, *Food in Chinese Culture,* the famous Harvard archaeologist Professor K. C. Chang confidently asserts that "the ancient Chinese were among the peoples of the world who have been particularly preoccupied with food and eating." He also quotes the eminent French Sinologue Jacques Gernet, who said, "There is no doubt that in this sphere China has shown a greater inventiveness than any other civilization."

As many have no doubt already realized, what is a hamantash after all but a form of dumpling? In China a dumpling is said to consist of two parts—the *pi*, the outer covering or skin, if you will, and the *xiar*, the filling. This description, it is safe to say, will be immediately recognizable to you as a description of the hamantash. Professor K. C. Chang in fact singles out the dumpling—and by extension the hamantash—as classic instantiations of what he calls "the *fan-cai* principle of Chinese food." At the base of the complex, interrelated variables involved in the preparation of food in Chinese culture is the division between *fan*, grains and other starch foods, and *cai*, vegetable, fruit or meat dishes. For a meal to be balanced, it must have an appropriate amount of both *fan* and *cai*. Grains are cooked whole or used as flour to constitute the *fan* part; vegetables and meats are cut up and mixed into individual dishes to constitute the *cai* half. To quote Professor Chang again: "Even in meals in which the staple starch portion and the meat, vegetable or fruit portion are apparently joined together such as in dumplings, steamed buns with fillings [and we may interject, hamantashen], they are in fact put together but not mixed up, and each still retains its due proportion and own distinction.

The Ancient Phase

We begin at the dawn of Chinese civilization. It is a little-known fact that the earliest known progenitor of the hamantash—what I call the archaic protohamantash—was invented between 1300 and 1000 BCE during the Shang dynasty, the first Chinese dynasty to leave behind written records, excised on oracle bones. Cow shoulder blades and tortoise carapaces were heated so that cracks emerged which could be deciphered for divination purposes. After the diviner had cracked the oracle bone, the crack was interpreted and an engraver then cut a record of the divination into the bones or shells. I am by no means an expert in this field. Tonight I simply offer to you one piece of evidence I have culled from the published oracle bone inscriptions. The inscription reads:

Preface: Crack making on day 16. Charge: "We will have prune/we will not perhaps have prune." Prognostication: The king reading the cracks said: "We will have prune; it will be on day 19." Verification: On day 19 we really did have prune." (The formulaic wording follows Keightley, Sources of Shang History.)

Though scholarly opinion has by no means reached a consensus whether this cryptic inscription actually refers to hamantashen, I want to point out that botanists long ago proved that the plum, apricot, and cherry all originated in East Asia; moreover, wheat was cultivated and consumed in the Central Chinese plain—the cradle of Chinese civilization and the Shang's domain—from very early on. This means that the botanical conditions for hamantashen were present in North China from earliest times, and therefore the strong likelihood that hamantashen were the topic of the king's divination cannot be ruled out. But for more solid evidence we must look a bit later, namely to the *Book of Odes,* traditionally attributed to Confucius, as editor, which would place it around 600 BCE during the Western Zhou dynasty. Let us consider Ode 20.

> Plop fall the plums, but there are still seven.
> Let those gentlemen that would court me
> Come while it is lucky!
> . . .
> Plop fall the plums; in shallow baskets we lay them. . . .
> [*Book of Songs*]

Here I believe we should follow the emendation of the great eighteenth-century philologist Dai Zhen, who argued that the text had been corrupted at this point. According to Dai, this line originally read, "Plop fall the plums; in shallow *pastries* we lay them." Also following Dai Zhen's lead, we reject the traditional Han dynasty allegorical interpretation of this poem that takes the plum as a metaphor for the ruler and the shallow baskets as a metaphor for the loyal ministers who surrounded him at court. I'm not sure, however, that I would go as far as another French Sinologue, Marcel Granet, who believes we can find traces in this poem of an ancient Chinese fertility cult suppressed by later Confucian exegetes. According to Granet, this fertility cult centered on the alleged aphrodisiac qualities of "plums in shallow pastries." But if Granet is correct, do we not have here incontrovertible textual evidence (from one of the five Confucian classics, no less) of the ancient Chinese hamantash?

Before moving on to our next phase, some speculations on the hamantash's original significance in Chinese cosmology are clearly in order. The triangular shape of the hamantash most likely symbolizes the triad of Heaven, Earth and Man, known as the *san cai* or "Three Powers." To a combination of the Three Powers are attributed the origin of the trigrams in the ancient divination manual, *The Yijing (I-Ching)*:

In ancient times the holy sages made the Book of Changes *thus: Their purpose was to follow the order of their nature and of fate. Therefore they determined the dao of heaven and called it the yin and yang. They determined the* dao *of earth and called it the yielding and firm. They determined the* dao *of man and called it humaneness and rectitude. They combined these three fundamental powers and doubled them; therefore, in the* Book of Changes *a sign is always formed by six lines (which we call hexagrams).*

Now I ask you to visualize a hamantash. While we usually describe a hamantash as a triangle, is it not more accurate to describe it as a triangle within a triangle, a triangle of filling nestled within an enveloping triangle of pastry? Could it not then be said of the hamantash that the holy sages combined the three powers and doubled them to echo the hexagrams of the *I-Ching*?

Confirmation of this hypothesis has recently been provided by a newly discovered manuscript of the *Book of Changes* from the Mawangdui tombs of the second century BCE. This text sheds significant light on the cosmic symbolism of the ancient Chinese hamantash, as you will see in the following quotation:

Confucius said: "The properties of the Changes *are only in the yin and yang, six lines creating a pattern. Being broken off in the middle of it, it is soft;*

*straight across, it is hard. Six hards without a soft is called the Great Yang; this
is the property of heaven. Six softs without a hard; this is the property of
earth. Heaven and earth embrace each other, vapor and flavor infuse each
other, the yin and yang flow into form, and the hard and soft complete."*

Certainly, the hamantash is what is being referred to here—the soft
fruit filling broken off in the middle of it, the hard pastry shell forming a pattern around it; the vapor and flavor of filling and pastry in-
fusing each other, as the yin and yang flowing into one another,
completing the hard and the soft.

The Early Modern Phase

Skipping over a millennium and a couple of centuries in our survey, we arrive at what I have called "the early modern phase" of Chinese hamantash development.

In the tenth and eleventh centuries the northern Song capital of
Kaifeng, and in the thirteenth century the southern Song capital of
Hangzhou, were the greatest cities in the world, a reputation due in
no large measure to their well-developed restaurant culture. These
included grand restaurants and teahouses as well as humbler noodle shops and wine joints. But it is among the ubiquitous take-out
food shops that we find the early modern versions of both hamantashen and latkes. The most common take-out shops sold *bing,* a
term that covers both sweet pastries such as *yuebing* (moon cakes)
and savory pancakes such as *congyou bing* (scallion pancakes), both
easily available in any Chinatown today. Shops in Kaifeng typically
specialized in one of two kinds of *bing*: sugared stuffed pastries or
fried pancakes. According to a thirteenth-century Chinese memoir
of the period, "The two most successful *bing* shops in Kaifeng both
had upward of fifty ovens" (*Food in Chinese Culture*, 158). Kaifeng, you
are probably aware, is the city in China most closely associated with
the Jews; even today a remnant Jewish population can be identified
there. While leading an American Jewish Congress tour to China recently, I went to Kaifeng, where I had the privilege of interviewing
several of these Chinese Jews. I am now persuaded that Kaifeng sup-
plies the missing link heretofore absent from histories of both Jewish and Chinese cuisine. Undoubtedly, Jewish traders carried these

early modern antecedents of the hamantash from Kaifeng across the arid desert of the Silk Road to Eastern Europe. That this important transcultural link has been virtually expunged from the historical record is due entirely to the defamations of anti-Sinites.

After the fall of the northern Song to the Jurchen, the southern Song capital of Hangzhou continued many of the food traditions of Kaifeng. Thus, when Marco Polo wrote that Hangzhou is the "greatest city which may be found in the world, where so many pleasures may be found that one fancies himself to be in Paradise" (quoted in *Food in Chinese Culture*), one of these pleasures was clearly food. Among these we must list the early modern forms of the latke and the hamantash. Although scholars now generally discredit the theory that Marco Polo brought back noodles from China to Italy, I suggest that one important new avenue for future scholarly research instead should be Marco Polo's role in introducing the hamantash (and perhaps the latke) to Europe.

At this stage in our inquiry, we must pause and ponder the following questions: Given that the Chinese were so technologically advanced in both the culinary and commercial sphere and so far ahead of the West in the manufacture of both hamantashen and latkes, what was it in the civilization that held the Chinese back from arriving at the true modern forms of these delicacies? To put it another way, what prevented these sprouts of capitalism from flowing into the hamantashen we know and love today? The "hamantash question," as it is known in the field, has been the driving force behind Joseph Needham's *Science and Civilization in China*; for those really interested in the hamantash's relationship to traditional Chinese chemistry, metallurgy, and hydraulic engineering, I refer you to volumes 8 through 10 of this magisterial work.

The Semi-Colonial, Semi-Imperial Phase

I move now to the nineteenth century, where we enter the shameful semi-colonial, semi-imperialist chapter of Chinese hamantash history. You all know the British Empire's situation at this time: domestic demand for imported Chinese tea was so great that the balance of trade was severely skewed, and British silver was flowing unchecked into China. What was an imperialist, colonialist nation to do? Wracking their brains for a product that the Chinese could be induced to import from them, the British hit upon the nefarious scheme of inculcating in the Chinese a dependence upon the poppy. And what better vehicle than the poppy-seed hamantash, whose addictive properties were only too well known in European scientific and diplomatic circles of the day? Although as I have demonstrated, China had from ancient times abounded in indigenous fruit-stuffed pastries (especially if you count red bean paste as a fruit), the country had ever lacked poppy-seed fillings. Soon the British had planted poppies on a vast scale in India and were dumping vast amounts of poppy seeds on the Chinese market. The plan worked perfectly. Before long, scores of Chinese had fallen prey to that terrible scourge known as hamantash addiction. Indeed this is one of the most vile and pernicious acts in world history, the deliberate enslavement and enfeeblement of an entire population to heavy pastries! Though the Chinese had always been fond of prune, apricot, and other varieties, the poppy-seed filling was virtually unknown in China until the coming of the West.

In Canton, the brave commissioner Lin Zexu could take it no longer and had the entire cargo of British-imported Indian poppy seeds publicly burned in the city square. The result, as you all know, was the Poppy Seed War of 1839–1842 (better but inaccurately known as the Opium War). This was followed some fifteen years later by the second Poppy Seed War, in which the French fought alongside the British. As you are aware, China lost both wars, which resulted in the unequal treaties, the forced opening of treaty ports to Western trade, and the cessation to Britain of Hong Kong. Naturally imports of poppy-seed hamantashen only increased during the second half of the nineteenth century, and soon you had on a vast scale the truly deplorable, truly disgusting spectacle of Chinese dissipating themselves in lurid hamantashen dens. The sad history of decline and decadence that followed is only too well known.

And when in the first decades of the twentieth century, White Russian Jewish refugees arrived in Shanghai and Harbin, they marveled at the glut of hamantashen they found on the market without realizing how this had come to be.

Thus the forced addiction to poppy-seed hamantashen by the Western imperialist powers is now considered one of the leading causes of the Chinese revolution. One of Chairman Mao's first acts when he took power in 1949 was to outlaw the hamantash habit in his countrymen. All hamantashen—the innocent prune and apricot along with the evil poppy seed—were eradicated from the new People's Republic, an accomplishment which the Chinese Communist Party has justifiably prided itself upon. One unfortunate consequence of this was that the poppy-seed trade in Asia simply migrated south beyond Chinese borders to Burma, Thailand, and Vietnam. It is from the hamantash of course that the region derived its nickname, "The Golden Triangle." More than twenty years after the death of Mao, however, we have learned that the hamantash was never fully eradicated from China after all, but survived in underground forms in certain remote rural areas under the name of *sanjiao*, or triangle—to be sure, as a much-reduced and impoverished pastry (with sugar rather than fruit as a filling). Even so, this exciting finding supports the thesis I advanced at the beginning of my lecture, namely that of all civilizations in the world, only the Chinese can claim an unbroken 3000-year-long hamantash history.

I am sorry to have neglected the doughty (or is it the stodgy?) latke's role in the history of Chinese civilization. But you have to realize that the festival of oil lasts not eight days but all year round in China. As a result, the latke's history is far less singular in East Asia and has garnered far less attention from scholars than that of the weightier hamantash. I nonetheless end my remarks with a plea that both the latke and the hamantash are indispensable to any serious understanding of Chinese culture; after all, you can't have all hamantashen and no latkes, just as you can't have yin without yang.

The Hamantash and the Foundation of Civilization; or, The Edible Triangle, the Oedipal Triangle, and the Interpretation of History

HAROLD T. SHAPIRO

I appear here tonight to restore the rightful place of the delectable hamantashen—mother of all Jewish pastries—into the mainstream of the history of ideas—really big ideas. For those who know the true but often forgotten story—in fact, a story so insidiously suppressed by a cabal of tuber-worshiping Latkovites—I ask you not to reveal it to your neighbors until I have outlined it in every fantastic and fabulous detail.

It turns out that although the impact of hamantashen on contemporary life and our understanding of history has been largely overlooked, it has been truly momentous. This fact is so little appreciated that on campuses all over the world students and faculty continue—inexplicably—to actually debate the relative merits of hamantashen and latkes as if the two, one a poorly disguised potato and the other a force in modern history, could seriously—or even in jest—truly be compared. No wonder some members of the public do not like what is happening on university campuses. After all—I ask you—what would the Maccabees have done with a latke? Recall also that in the Jewish tradition such a question is itself the answer.

To understand the little-known and little-understood power of hamantashen, I have to ask you to let your minds go back to Europe of the nineteenth century and especially Vienna in the late nineteenth and early twentieth centuries. Recall that Marx and Darwin had already done their best to unmask the pretensions of the Victorian era by pointing out that we, despite our vaunted rationality, were all unwitting participants in a grand historical drama that, prior to their prophetic insights, we barely understood. That is, things in the human and animal kingdoms, whether biological (Darwin) or sociological (Marx), were just not what they appeared to be.

It was left to Freud, however, working in Vienna early in this century, to finally unmask us all and reveal the true underlying secret of our personalities, our history and all those institutions, practices, and traditions we call civilization. As you will see in a moment, it is here that the celebration of Purim and the power of hamantashen come in.

In any case, Freud's ideas regarding the interpretation of history and personality were so powerful that they swept across the West like a great tidal wave—a tidal wave whose origins all too many scholars (and, here, sadly, I cannot exempt members of our own faculty from this charge) have wrongly traced to Greek antiquity. The Latke-Hamantash Debate would be little more than an entertainment if it were not for the powerful role, not of heathen Greece and Rome, but of the hamantash in Freud's thinking. Our received wisdom regarding the origins of Freud's interpretation of history is a neurotic, perhaps even psychotic, illusion which Freud himself mistakenly shared and which must be overcome, or as Freud might say—sublimated. The fact is, to continue with the sophisticated language of psychoanalysis—it may be Greek to him, but it's hamantash to me. Let me explain.

For those of you not intimately familiar with Freud's work, let me remind you all that in his magnificent opus *Civilization and Its Discontents*, Freud made the Oedipal Triangle the historical and emotional foundation of culture, law, civility, and decency. To become a little more technical for a moment, Freud actually proposed that the Oedipal Triangle, and certain other sexual matters, were the underlying primal forces that shaped both personal and large-scale history! For those of you unfamiliar with the idea of the Oedipal Triangle, sometimes known as the Oedipal Complex, it refers to the incestuous impulses of a child for the parent of the opposite sex, and the child's murderous impulses for the other parent; this makes the child feel guilty and induces the formation of the superego, which then makes possible the very idea of civilized life.

Thus, every new arrival on the planet is faced with the task of either mastering the Oedipal Triangle by adopting a civilized superego, or of descending into barbarism. Freud's Jewish mother—as all Jewish mothers before her—knew that guilt, the true lubricating oil of civilization, was the essential weapon in the great struggle against all uncivilized tendencies, and necessary for the sublimation of sexual energies. Indeed, Freud suggested that it was this sense of guilt that provided the energy for the advance of civilization. Big surprise! This has been the rallying cry of Jewish mothers from Sarah, Rebecca, Rachel, and Leah all the way to Joan Rivers, and there is no use denying the power of this idea. It took Freud, however, to bring it out to our secular consciousness.

Now what has all this to do with Purim? Just about everything, for the fact is that Freud's great theory came not because he was consuming too many latkes—a rather laughable notion—but because he was celebrating in rather too grand a fashion the month of Adar. Adar, as we know, is a month when we celebrate the transformation of darkness into light, and it is this aspect of the month that was so attractive to Freud, who usually paid little attention to Jewish traditions.

Freud was fascinated by the transformation of things from their apparent reality—or socially constructed illusion—to their underlying true nature. Adar, he thought, was a great example of such transformation, since what seemed to be sadness and desolation really was gladness and celebration. In those ancient days of Esther, as today, things were not what they seemed to be.

And so it came to pass that one year in the month of Adar, Sigmund attended a special Purim masked ball. It was on this historic night that Freud, in a most celebratory mood, ate rather too many hamantashen made with rather too many poppy seeds, which, even in those days, was a controlled substance. He then fell into a deep sleep and had a strange dream. In his dream, he was wandering through a performance of Sophocles' *Oedipus Rex*—that vivid drama of love, murder, intrigue, and the search for truth. This is not so surprising since *Oedipus* means "swollen," and so was Freud's stomach. In any case, he noticed almost immediately that everyone was wearing masks! This must mean, he thought, that they were also celebrating Purim and, therefore, given that it must be the month of Adar, he knew that things were not what they seemed to be! He quickly recognized that Oedipus of Thebes, like the members of his own Viennese society, was quite unable to see the true nature of things.

When Freud awoke, a mysterious force sent him directly to his study and he wrote *Civilization and Its Discontents*. Unfortunately for future generations, and numerous contemporary literary critics, his initial interpretation of the dream was still floating somewhere between his conscious and unconscious state, and he failed to realize that it was the power of hamantashen that had, at a most propitious moment, showed him how Sophocles' drama held the clue to all of history.

In Freud's conscious memory of the dream he mistook Sophocles' Oedipal Triangle for the Edible Triangle of Purim—the hamantash—and thus came to a completely erroneous view of the true origins of his interpretation of civilization. Through the mysterious role of transference, he mistakenly attributed the primal force of Purim's Edible Triangle—the hamantash—to Sophocles' Oedipal Triangle. In all fairness, we might forgive this error, since he had no analyst to help him interpret his dream, and its origins, properly.

Hence, from that time to this we have continued to cling to this unfortunate illusion, and in the shadowy mists of history, we have lost sight of the importance of Purim and the influence of the consumption of hamantashen in generating creative energy within Freud that enabled him, and now all of us, to suddenly understand clearly the dynamics of all history. Moreover, the consumption of hamantashen has the potential to release the same creative energy in any of us.

While many believe that all of history, and most of literary criticism, is propelled by a complex mixture of incestuous desires, murderous desires, other sexual concerns, and especially guilt, perhaps history, like hamantashen, is simply a mixture of eggs, flour, salt, baking powder, sugar, fruit, and especially poppy seeds, whatever else it might seem to be.

As we look to the future, particularly at a university where creative energy and the search for truth is at a premium, let us both praise and devour hamantashen, for that will not only replace the guilt and its supposedly civilizing influence, but cause us to completely forget the hopeless and insidious latke!

The Archetypal Hamantash:
A Feminist Mythology; An Exercise in the History of Religious Methodology

WENDY DONIGER

In prehistoric times (or, as we say, *in illo tempore*), all societies were matriarchies, of course, and worshiped the Feminine in the form of a hamantash. But when the Indo-European male-chauvinist pigs (unclean goyim) destroyed the civilizations in which the Goddess reigned, they replaced Her with their male gods, and they replaced Her sacred Hamantashen with their profane latkes. I will argue that the religions of the ancient Near East and the religions of India had a single ancestor, a Hamantash-Goddess-worshiping primitive tribe, of which the traces have been carefully trampled out in Judaism but still survive in Hinduism. More specifically, I will demonstrate beyond any shadow of a doubt that the sacred prune (particularly when enveloped in a womb-like pastry) was the symbol of the female's androgynous ability to procreate unilaterally and "bring forth," and that it was replaced by the profane potato, which was, particularly when "bound up" with egg, the symbol of the male's frustrated incapacity to bring forth and of his consequent womb-envy and misogyny.

The present form of the potato latke gives no clue as to its original sexual symbolism, but fortunately we can reconstruct the hypothetical archetypal Latke, which was indubitably male: it was a potato pancake, but one formed more like a crêpe, and it was rolled (like the crêpe) into a long, phallic tube, filled with *smetene* (sour cream) or butter (both common ritual symbols of semen); it is most likely that the potato latke once had a sacred role as the ritual counterpart of the mythic bullrushes in which Moses was found (themselves phallic symbols, as Otto Rank has shown). Thus the form of the latke was once male. Its content is still male, for although the gender of the potato may seem irrelevant or at least indeterminable, the other basic ingredient in the latke is positively macho: eggs, a well-known slang term for testicles in most Indo-European languages (*yaitsi* in Russian), including, of course, Yiddish (*eier*).

The Indian latke, called the *chapati*, often made with potatoes, is the symbol of royalty and male dominance; this is clear from a tale told of the emperor Chandragupta Maurya in the third century BC: while debating within himself about how to conquer India, he saw an Indian mother telling her child to eat his *chapati* from the outside, where it would cool faster: "Adasva, adasva, tata," she said (the exact Sanskrit equivalent of the Yiddish, *Ess, ess, tatele*). From his observation of the mother (who was, significantly, harassing her son to make him eat), Chandragupta conceived the idea of beginning his campaign by harassing the outlying provinces, rather than staging a palace coup at the center, and with this decision the emperor was on his way to victory. So much for the macho latke.

The analysis of the hamantash turns upon the sensitive issue of the relationship between form and content. In form, the hamantash is a womb, a container; in form, it is an archetypal symbol of the female. But the rich complexity of the hamantash lies in the variety of its manifestational contents: sometimes it is filled with poppy seed, sometimes with cherry, and sometimes with prunes. The cherry is another symbol of the female, more specifically, of the female virgin; the poppy seed is, both in form (seed being a metaphor for semen) and in name (poppy, father), male. The prune mediates between these two polarized symbols; it is androgynous. When we have the prune in the pastry womb, we have the female androgyne, the woman with the power to create independent of any male, parthenogenetically (remember the virginal cherry). (This ancient androgynous paradigm survived in a degraded form, as Eliade would have put it, when one of the first people to undergo a surgical change of sex, Christine Jorgensen, was referred to as the Prune Danish, a term that Shakespeare had already applied to his most Oedipal character, Hamlet, "the melancholy [= dark-humored, i.e., prune-colored] Dane." The prune hamantash is thus the symbol of the archetypal androgynous Goddess and must have been the original hamantash. When the matriarchy was overthrown, the Mother was split into two halves, male (poppy) and female (cherry). It is typical of the male dominance in Jewish culture that the poppy hamantashen by far outnumber the cherry hamantashen.

There is a telling passage in English literature in which the prune and the potato appear together as symbols of the female and the male. This is a chapter from Dickens's *Little Dorrit*, in which Amy (whose older sister is named *Fanny*, believe it or not) addresses her father as "Father" and is told to call him "Papa" instead. Mrs. General, who makes the correction, goes on to remark, "Papa, potatoes, poultry, prunes, and prism are all very good words for the lips: especially prunes and prism." Now, for Papa and potatoes to be linked is of course inevitable (one need merely point out, in passing, the use of *poppy* seeds in the male forms of hamantashen). As for the other side, poultry symbolizes women, more precisely whores (*poules* in French). The final term, *prism*, is clearly a euphemism (or misprint, or scribal error, or late variant) for priapism. "Especially prunes and priapism," is surely what Dickens meant to say, expressing the primeval coupling of the female and male principles.

With this morphology in place, we can begin to investigate the history of the latke and the hamantash.

Let us look first at the book of Genesis. This is not the occasion to review in detail the complex and still unresolved argument about the actual botanical identity of the fruit that Eve gave Adam to eat. (One might point out, in passing, that the male chauvinist bias of Genesis is already revealed by the assumption that Eve, rather than Adam, will provide all the meals. Doubtless she rejoiced to find the fruit "good for food," as she must have been driven to desperation by Adam's repeated complaints: "What, figs for dinner again?"). The fruit, as we shall see, is the prune. The one remaining trace of this in the bowdlerized Hebrew text is the serpent's statement "In the day ye eat thereof, then your eyes shall be opened." This is a misreading, or a euphemism, or a scribal error, reading "your eyes" (*énichem*) for what must have been the original: "bowels" (*mé echem*). "Then your *bowels* shall be opened." It is but the work of a moment to emend the Hebrew text, revealing one of the earliest expressions of the Jewish obsession with laxatives. This obsession recurs, obsessively, throughout the Hebrew Bible: David sat for forty years, we are told, and Baalam had a stubborn ass.

This passage also demonstrates the male chauvinist bias, for, as we shall see, anal creation (or "creative cloaca," as it is sometimes called) is the quintessential expression of male pregnancy envy. For Adam and Eve were originally an androgyne, from which God removed Eve, the female soul from the male body, in the form of a rib (the earliest biblical reference to soul food). Adam thus longs to return to the primordial state of fecund androgyny (just as, in Plato's *Symposium*, some males long to unite with females in order to regain their lost androgyny). Further support for this interpretation is offered by yet another line in the Hebrew text: after Eve and Adam have eaten the fruit, Eve is cursed to bring forth children "in pain and travail" (*etsev*), and Adam is cursed to eat food "in toil" (*itsavon*). These two phrases are derived from the same verb and represent the same physiological function, "straining" or "bearing down," as both the woman on the obstetrical table and the child on the potty are encouraged to do. The role of the prune in facilitating both of these processes need not be further labored. The fact that later generations glossed the fruit as an apple is the result of a double bowdlerization by male commentators; when the prune cult was overthrown, the fruit in Eden was said to be a potato, symbol of the stopped-up (anally retentive) male. The French for potato is *pomme de terre*, "apple of the earth" (earth being of course a symbol of the Goddess). As the centuries went by, male (or careless) scribes left off the final chthonic, female phrase, and the fruit was said to be simply a *pomme*, or apple. It is surely worth noting that the French name for the latke in its original tubal form (*crêpe*) reveals the fecal symbolism clearly enough, if we merely view the word as a French imitation of the English slang for feces, pronounced, appropriately, with a Yiddish accent: *crep*. (A similar point could be made with regard to *krep*lakh —also a womb-imitation food, well known to be frightening to male children). Thus feces are a surrogate for the male's lost power of procreation, and the prune is needed, ironically, as a laxative to release the fecal "progeny" of the male who is bound up by the very potato that he had used to dethrone the *ur*-prune.

The fracas in Eden is repeated in a Mesopotamian story that resurfaces in the tale of Esther, the triumph of the archetypal earth-goddess Ishtar (who becomes Esther) over the powers of evil, Hum-man or Humbar or Humbaba (who becomes Haman). Again, the prune is not mentioned by name (probably because, like the name of God in the Hebrew text, it was too sacred to say out loud), but this need not trouble us. Esther seduces and kills Haman as Eve se-duced and undid Adam (and all Jewish mothers seduce their con-sort-sons, by *feeding* them; the lighthearted phrase, "Help yourself t' a piece *fruit*" has deeply sinister implications that have been re-pressed for millennia). Esther invites Haman to a banquet and feeds him something that reduces him to putty in her hands. This event is commemorated at Purim by the eating of the archetypal haman-tash, for Esther consumes Haman as we consume the hamantash, in an inverted eucharist expressing the devouring of the demonic enemy. We shall return to Haman later. First, let us further explore this prune complex, which explains for the first time why haman-tashen are eaten at the feast of Purim.

The prune as the symbol of the seductive, dangerous woman per-sists in Western civilization. In Shakespeare's *Measure for Measure*, the wife of the constable Elbow wanders into a whorehouse "great with child; and longing, saving your honours' reverence, for stewed prunes" (II.1.88). This passage reflects the ancient belief that a preg-nant woman might long for certain forbidden fruits (prunes, in the Ugaritic tradition, and pickles and ice cream in the Hittite); more-over, she would send her husband to procure these fruits, often at the cost of his life. (Eve's behavior in Eden is a structural reversal of this theme: she gives *him* the fruit, and she gets pregnant as a *re-sult* of eating it. This variant, like the original of which it is an in-version, is widespread.) The particular reference in *Measure for Mea-sure* is to stewed prunes, "the staple dish offered in bawdy houses," with a further play on "stewed," applied to the inmates. This use of emetics in whorehouses is but one form of the universal belief that sexually voracious women "bleed a man to death," "drain his vital fluids," "suck him dry," and so forth. All of these fantasies and pho-bias are refocused in Judaism upon the central anal fixation, and the wicked woman wields not the castrating knife but the enema tube. This tube, a phallic symbol in its own right, is the sign of Aphrodite with a phallus, as is clear from the Babylonian creation epic, the *Enema Elish*. (The ancient Jewish terror of this procedure reemerged

in the twentieth century in the term applied to the massacres per-
petrated in the name of the great international Jewish Communist
conspiracy: the Stalinist *purges* of the *Trots*kyites.)

In India, the archetypal prune is far more prominent than it is in
the West. Much has been written about the sacred plant of the *Rig
Veda*, the Soma. Some benighted souls have even gone so far as to attempt to demonstrate that Soma was a hallucinogenic mushroom (a
phallic symbol throughout the world). This hypothesis represents yet
again the superimposition of male models on female intuitions. Soma
is indeed mind-altering, but in a female mode, in the sense that the
sacred prune "altered the mind" of Adam and Haman: it bewitches
through the power of the Eternal Feminine, exciting the misogynist
envy of the power to procreate even while it weakens the man by
draining his vital fluids. Soma is a dried prune. The *Rig Veda* clearly
establishes the fact that Soma was dried, preserved, and served to the
(male) gods when it had been infused and cooked—that is, stewed.

One particular passage demonstrates not only the identity of
Soma as a prune but its significance as a symbol of male pregnancy
envy and anal creation:

*Indra, the king of the gods, was excluded by the other gods from drinking Soma
juice, but uninvited he consumed the Soma, taking it by force. It hurt him:
it flowed in all directions from his vital openings; only from his mouth it did
not flow. From what flowed from the nose there sprang a lion; from his ears,
a wolf; from his anus, the tigers and other wild beasts, and from his urinary
opening a foaming spirit. He spat three times, producing three kinds of ju-
jube berries. When he was thus purged by Soma, he walked about tottering,
until the celestial physicians cured him.*

This is indeed a rich passage. We begin with the definition of
Soma as the forbidden fruit and of Indra as the uninvited guest, like
Adam, the archetypal *schnorrer* (a persistent devil in Jewish folklore).
Indra then succumbs to the first recorded case of Delhi belly, an excessive "purging" caused by an excess of prunes. Finally, the theme
of the doctor as savior appears, the source of the Jewish cultural reverence (or, rather, of the Jewish *mother's* reverence) for the medical
profession as the shamanic controllers of prunes. The ancient Hindu
terror of excessive purging, however, was counterbalanced by an

equal terror of constipation, so that the ancient Hindus fell between two stools, as it were. Thus the celibate sage Cyavana was pelted with balls of cow shit by naughty boys; a later version of this story states that, in revenge, Cyavana put a curse of constipation on the men of that land.

Hindus, like Jews, have always been, and still are, remarkably concerned with their bowels. The Hindu gods create anally: Brahma eats rice and then emits us, and he created the demons (Asuras) in the form of a breath (*asu*) from his rectum. Thus man is a cosmic turd, and though the theological implications are not entirely clear, demons would appear to be of less consequence, or at least less substance—no more than a celestial fart. In Greek tradition, so closely related to the Sanskrit, the "purging" effect of prunes was replaced by the important concept of *catharsis*, the inner cleansing of the soul, accomplished by the witnessing of a Greek tragedy. The original, physiological nature of this *catharsis* is echoed in the notorious incident in Aristophanes' *Frogs*, where Dionysus himself, the patron god of tragedy, in terror defecates in his pants.

Alan Dundes has written much about anal creation, as it appears, for instance, in the myth of the earth-diver, who plunges down into the mud (or *drek*—a euphemism for feces) and makes the universe out of dirt (a process that has been termed "scatological eschatology"). The interchangeability of feces and dirt is central to the myths of the Hindu god Ganesha (Lord of Ganiffs), who is usually said to be created from dirt rubbed off his mother's body (Ganesha is *very* fond of his mommy, and even keeps Daddy out of the bedroom) but is also occasionally created, in myth and in ritual, out of cow dung— the feces of the mother. Dundes, a self-confessed Freudian, has glossed this as expressive of the male's envy of the woman's ability to create, and of his fantasy of creating not through a womb (which he lacks) but through the anus.

These myths of male anal creation are linked, in India as in ancient Israel, with myths of the forbidden fruit and lost androgyny. In order for a Hindu woman to become pregnant, she is given a consecrated bowl of food to eat; this is a mixture of rice (the Hindu answer to poppy seed) and milk—a kind of androgynous rice pudding. In folk tales, the woman is given a mango (a later Hindu variant of the *ur*-prune). Now, in several ancient Hindu myths, a man eats the food consecrated for his wife—the forbidden prune—and becomes pregnant, whereupon he eventually gives birth anally or in some other arcane manner. In one variant of these myths, a pregnant goddess desires a nonbotanical "forbidden fruit": she wishes to have fun with other men at a party, but she is too great with child to go out. Her accommodating husband takes the embryo into his own body; she goes off, meets someone who takes her fancy, and never returns; nine months later the husband, unable to deliver the child, dies. Thus the ancient, life-giving, laxative powers of the prune in the cult of the Hamantash Goddess are twisted into poisonous powers of constipation—female creative powers, that is, that become deadly when imitated by the male.

The pregnant male is filled: *pleine*, as the French so rudely say of a pregnant woman, or "stuffed"—like a pastry—in the English obscenity. For the Hindu goddess, to be full (*pur*) is to be full of food: thus the Goddess is Anna Purna, the Goddess Full of Food, or (through the simple transposition of the *r* and the *n*), Anna Pruna, Our Lady of the Prunes. This root—*pur*—(that we have already encountered in the English verb, to *purge* or make un-full) appears in several different cultural contexts bound together in the latke-hamantash complex.

The Indian bread that corresponds to the hamantash (in contrast with the *chapati*, the Indian latke), a puffed, pastry-like bread that can be stuffed, is the *puri*, from the same root as *pur* in Anna Purna. And this same verbal root plays a central role in the Jewish context, in *Pur*im, the feast of the hamantash, establishing finally and beyond any possible doubt the parallelism of the Sanskritic, Semitic, and semiotic mythic traditions. When we feed this insight back into the tale of Esther, we realize that Haman died not because he envied *Mordecai*, the mentor of Esther, as the extant text lamely but repeatedly insists, but rather because, in the original lost version, the reconstructed *ur*-text, he envied *Esther*. The little three-cornered prune cakes preserve, in their innocent folk wisdom, the true meaning of the original, for though they are said (unconvincingly) to represent the *hat* of Haman, *tasche* does not mean "hat"; it means "pocket." More precisely, it is a euphemism for the female sexual organ (as when a seductive woman is said to have a man "in her pocket"). Haman died giving birth, in a pitiful attempt to work out his envy of Esther, the archetypal goddess who had Haman in her pocket.

Noshes

I begin with mathematics, and call to your attention the fundamental issue of the geometrical shape of the latke (the circle) and the shape of the hamantash (a triangle). What has not been realized is that the latke-hamantash relation—that is the circle/triangle conjunction—is precisely the underlying shape of the most fundamental transformative patterns in the material world. When one joins together the circle and triangle, one arrives at a two-dimensional cone, a dynamic shape that immediately suggests a head and a tail, and therefore a direction of movement. (It is no accident, of course, that the latke is the head, the brains of the organism; what that makes of the hamantash I will leave to your imagination.) When a turn or rotation is added to this figure, the head tends to chase its own tail, and produce the eternal cycle of life as reflected in the diagram of the great yin-yang symbol.

If time permitted, I would unfold for you the entire cosmological significance of the latke-hamantash dialectic, revealing it as the fundamental structure of the universe in ancient religious thought. As the great ziggurat of Ur, for instance, spirals upward from its round, latke-ish foundations toward the heavens, it inevitably creates a structure that reminds us of the hamantash. Indeed, the basic structures of the celestial and terrestrial universes, from the starry nebula to the oceanic maelstrom to the underlying structure of life itself, are traceable to the conjunction of opposites revealed in the latke-hamantash relation. Since I do not have time to demonstrate all these points in the mathematical detail they deserve, I would simply ask you to clear your minds and meditate, allowing the cosmic force of the sacred latke to drive the darkness and ignorance—that is, the hamantash—from your mind. TOM MITCHELL, *The Cosmological Significance of the Latke-Hamantash Dialectic*

✡   ✡   ✡

A cryptic grave marker in Rome dating from 114 BCE clearly establishes that hamantashen were made in Rome before 114. This marker notes that Publius Cato was a senator, etc., etc., and then at the very end is the cryptic (pardon the pun) note: "He held the secret of the poppy seed triad and thus was greatly enriched." What could be clearer? It is evident that Publius had somehow come into possession of the hamantash recipe—how, we'll never know—probably through some merchant from Jerusalem. BERNARD S. SILBERMAN, *Hamantashen and the Roman Empire*

✡   ✡   ✡

It has been established by the most careful research that the word "latke" derives from the Sanskrit *latsha* (large number), which in Hindu became *lakhe*, meaning 100,000 rupees. And indeed the word was used in the diary of a Spanish Jew in his voyages with Columbus in search of the wealth of the Indies. However, when instead of the wealth of the Indies, he brought back only the lowly Haitian *batata* (Spanish, *patata*), it became the in joke among educated Sephardim that *patata lakhe* (literally, potato money) is the wealth of the Indies. Hence the custom of making potato latkes in the shape of Spanish Pieces of Eight. RICHARD LASHOF, *Origins of the Latke and the Hamantash*

✡   ✡   ✡

It is well known that the major breadstuff in Mexico and Guatemala is the tortilla, which is a latke made not of grated potatoes but of grated—or ground—maize. One obvious conclusion that might be drawn is that this lends credence to the theory that the American Indians originated as one of the lost tribes of Israel. On the contrary, the Jews may well have come originally from Guatemala. SOL TAX, *The Tribe of Israel*

TRY 'EM, YOU'LL LIKE 'EM

Lovely, Luscious Latkes

Of course, no one makes latkes like Momma. The grating, the making, the smells and the mess are what memories are made of: oil splattering, potatoes turning black, shredded skin in the batter, kitchen smoky, Momma frying a new batch of latkes while everyone in the other room eats them as fast as she can make them. Sodden, heavy, crispy, delicious, smothered with sour cream, sometimes smelling of *shmaltz*. Ah, those were the days! It's not clear that Momma's memories are quite as pleasant, but it is always good to have the family around, and so grate and fry she must, and does. Eat, eat, my children.

In consideration of those Mommas (and Poppas) who'd like to be out there eating crispy latkes with the rest of the family, the following recipe suggests how this can happen.

LATKES
(Makes about 28 potato pancakes, 2–3 inches each)

2   pounds russet (baking) potatoes, peeled and placed in a bowl of cold water
⅓   cup grated onion
2   eggs, lightly beaten (1 egg per pound of potatoes)*
1   cup all-purpose flour (best) or ½ cup matzah meal**

*   Too many eggs will overwhelm the taste of potato.
** Too much starch will make the latkes heavy. Use only about ½ cup flour or ¼ cup matzah meal per pound of potatoes—just enough to bind the mixture. If doubling the recipe, add flour slowly; the full amount may not be needed. Toward the end, the mixture gets very loose. It is better to release the extra liquid by squeezing it on a spoon rather than by adding more flour.

1   teaspoon salt, plus additional to taste
    Freshly ground black pepper to taste
    Peanut or canola oil for frying

* * *

1. Line a large baking sheet with paper towels. If not serving the latkes immediately—out of the frying pan into the dining room—preheat the oven to 200 degrees. Have a large bowl of cold water ready.
2. Grate the potatoes, using a hand grater or food processor fitted with the medium shredding disc. As potatoes are grated, transfer them to the bowl of water. When all of the potatoes are grated, set aside for 5 minutes. Drain the shredded potatoes in a large colander, rinsing with cold water. Transfer to a clean bowl.
3. Add the onion, the eggs, flour, salt, and pepper. Thoroughly combine the mixture.
4. In a large, preferably straight-sided pan, add oil to a depth of ¼ to ⅓ inch. Heat oil until a shred of potato dropped in the oil sizzles immediately.
5. Form pancakes, using 2 tablespoons from a regular silverware set. Scoop up a generous spoonful of the potato mixture with one spoon, flatten the mixture with the other spoon. Slide the latke into the oil. Repeat until the pan is full, but not crowded. Cook the latkes until browned at the edges. Turn the latkes over and cook until fully browned. Transfer the finished latkes to the lined baking sheet to drain excess oil. Repeat with the remaining mixture.
6. If not serving the latkes immediately, transfer the sheet to the pre-heated oven to keep warm. If serving even later, set the latkes aside to cool to room temperature, then freeze until ready to serve. Reheat the latkes in a 350-degree oven, and drain again on paper towels because reheating will release more oil.
    Serve with sour cream or applesauce. Add salt to taste.

Hamantashen Fit for an Ex-Queen

As the Latke-Hamantash Debate demonstrates, even those who fight together for the honor of the hamantash can come to blows over the matter of the best filling. The traditionalists (conservatives?) look askance at anything but poppy seed or prune, and argue over which of these is most destined for this delicate pastry. Others prefer cherry, apricot, or apple, but even these innovations are rejected by the modern *apikoros*, the child raised in America who sees chocolate as the only possible substance that should be stuffed inside the hamantash.

And then there is the other eternal question: cake or cookie dough? On the Web today one can find countless combinations of dough and filling, and the problem is compounded: which is the true hamantash? How elusive reality, how enduring the quest to understand the Divine plan!

Ex-Queen Vashti, who walked away from a life of ease in the palace of Shushan, Persia, long ago, thereby paving the way for Esther's ascendancy and the salvation of the Jews, reminds us of what is important in life, aside from hamantashen. Vashti refused to be degraded and disgraced by parading around like a Persian Miss America before her husband's drunken friends, and maintained her dignity and independence in the face of male oppression. In honor of this early feminist, Robin Leidner, University of Pennsylvania, offers her special Liberation Hamantashen.

LIBERATION HAMANTASHEN
(Makes about 24)

- ¾ cup sugar
- 2 cups sifted flour
- 2 teaspoons baking powder
- ¼ teaspoon salt
- ½ cup shortening
- 1 egg, beaten
- 2 tablespoons orange juice
- 1 17-ounce jar prune butter (*lekvar*). Can also use poppy seeds (*mohn*), apricot filling, or cherry pie filling.

* * *

1. Sift the sugar, flour, baking powder, and salt into a bowl. Work in the shortening by hand. Add the egg and orange juice, mixing until dough is formed. Chill overnight if possible, or at least two hours.

2. Roll out the dough about ⅛ inch thick on a lightly floured board. Cut into 3-inch circles (a teacup works). Place one heaping teaspoonful of the filling in each. Pinch three edges of the dough together (use a knife or spatula to lift the edges), but leave a small opening in the center; the resulting pastry will be in the shape of a triangle with a little of the filling showing. Place on a greased cookie sheet. Cover with a cloth and set aside for ½ hour.

3. Preheat the oven to 400 degrees. Baste hamantashen with beaten egg for a shinier crust, if desired. Bake hamantashen for about 20 minutes, or until delicately browned on top.

GLOSSARY

Adar (H) The twelfth month of the Jewish calendar. Purim is celebrated on the fourteenth of Adar.

Akiba, Akiva Outstanding scholar who lived in Palestine CE 50–135. Because he defied the Roman law against teaching the Torah, he was executed by the Romans.

aleph, bet, gimmel, dalid First letters of the Hebrew alphabet, corresponding to a, b, g, d

apikoros (H) Unbeliever, skeptic, heretic

Ashkenazic (H) Jew from Europe (Ashkenaz = Germany); Yiddish-speaking Jews

Ba'al Na'alyim Tovim A parodic term. Master of the Good Shoes

Ba'al Shem Tov (Master of the Good Name) (H). Common name for Israel ben Eliezer, founder of Chasidism, who lived in Podolia, Ukraine, from 1700 to 1760

balagan (Israeli slang) A mess, a muddle

bialy (Y) Flat breakfast roll, reputedly from Bialystok

bina (H) Understanding

blintzes (from Ukrainian) Filled crêpes, usually stuffed with cheese

borsht (Slavonic) Beet soup from Eastern Europe

bubbeh (Y) Grandmother

bubbeh-myseh (H) Nonsense, old wives' tale

bulkele, bulkelach (Y) A baked roll

challeh (Y from H) Braided loaf of egg bread, customary on the Sabbath and holidays

Chasidim (H) "Pious ones"; followers of the Ba'al Shem Tov, who sparked a Jewish revival movement in Eastern Europe emphasizing joy and piety in worship; Lubavitcher Chasidim are one of several branches of Chasidim. *Chasidic* adj.

chochem (Y from H) Wise, learned, or clever person

chochma (Y from H) Wisdom

cholent (Y) Meat and vegetable stew eaten on the Sabbath

chometz (Y from H) Leavened bread or other foods prohibited on Passover

chutzpah (Y from H) Brazen nerve, effrontery

da'at (H) Knowledge

dag gadol (H) Big fish (as in Jonah)

"Di-aynnu" (H) Song sung at the Passover seder, meaning "It would have been enough for us."

dreidl, dreidel (Y) Top that is spun on Hanukkah

drek (Y) Excrement; trash; worthless thing

etrog (H) A citrus fruit, one of the Four Species used with the myrtle, the palm, and the willow, during the fall festival of Succot. The *etrog* was a common Jewish symbol in ancient times.

eyn horeh (Y from H) Evil eye; *keyn eyn horeh*, magical phrase to ward off the evil eye

farfel (Y) Noodles

farvoszhe (Y) Why?

fleishedik (Y) Foods made with meat or meat products

fresser (Y) Glutton. *Fressn* is what animals do; *essn*, what people (are supposed to) do.

Galitzianer (Y) A Jew from Galicia, a province of southern Poland (mostly Austrian-Hungarian)

gantze megillah (Y) A big deal; the whole story

gatkes (Y) Underpants

gefilte (Y) Filled, as in gefilte fish

gelt (Y) Money

greps (Y) A belch

Hashem (H) The name; used to refer to God

Havdalah (H) Separation; twilight ritual separating the Sabbath from the rest of the week

Hillel Rabbinic authority and great teacher of the first century BCE, in Palestine, who exerted a major influence on the development of Judaism. Hillel's more lenient approach to the Law contrasted with the teachings of Shammai, and prevailed in Jewish thought.

homntash Yiddish pronunciation of "hamantash"

in dr'erd (Y) To hell; go to the devil

Kabbala, kabbalistic (H) Jewish mystical tradition

kashe (Y) Buckwheat groats

Khanuke Yiddish pronunciation of "Hanukkah"

khaveyrim (H) Friends, comrades

kishke (Y) Intestine; or, as food, intestine casing stuffed with a combination of meat, flour, and spices

Kislev The ninth month of the Jewish calendar. Hanukkah begins on the twenty-fourth of Kislev.

klipeh (Y) A shrew; an evil spirit

knaydl, knaydlekh (Y) Dumpling, especially dumplings made of matzah meal; matzah balls, used in chicken soup

knish (Y) Pastry stuffed with meat, potato, or spinach

kreplakh (Y) Dumpling of meat or cheese, usually put in soup

kugel, kugl (Y) Pudding

lechvar (Turkish) Prune filling for pastry like hamantashen

Litvak (Y) Person from Lithuania or neighboring areas, often considered rationalistic and humorless

lokshen kugel, lukshn kugl (Y) Noodle pudding

macher (Y) A big shot, an organizer, an "operator"

maneshtana, maneshthana (H) First words of the Four Questions posed during the Passover seder, asking, "Why is this night different from all other nights?"

matse-meyl (Y) Matzah meal

matzah (H), *matse* (Y) Unleavened bread eaten during Passover

matzah ball (E) Matzah meal dumpling, *knaydl*

mechaiyeh (Y from H) A great pleasure, a real joy

megillah (H) Scroll; Megillah Esther is the Scroll (or Book) of Esther read on Purim.

meshugge (Y) Crazy, silly, absurd

milchedik (H) Milk or milk-based foods

mishegass (Y) Nonsense, insanity, craziness

mitzvot (H) Divine principles, commandments, ethical and moral laws; acts of human kindness

mohn (Y) Poppy seeds

moror (H) Bitter herbs

Nisan The first month of the Jewish calendar. Passover begins on the fourteenth of Nisan.

noodnik, nudnik (Y) A pest; a colossal bore; an annoying person

nosh, nash (Y) A bite, small bit of food

oneg Shabbat (H) Enjoyment of the Sabbath, or evening gathering to honor the Sabbath

pareve (H) Neutral food, can be eaten with milk or meat

Pesach (H), *Peysakh* (Y) Passover

Pesachdik (H) Food permitted on Passover

pirogen (Y) Meat pies

ptcha (Y) Gelatin made by boiling calves' hooves and flavored with garlic

Purimspiel (Y) Purim dramatic play that is a humorous reflection on serious subjects

rasha (H) Evil person

Rashi Rabbi Solomon Yitzhaki (1040–1105), French biblical and rabbinic commentator. Rashi is renowned for his lucid commentaries, which are studied to this day.

Riboyne shel Oylem (Y from H) "Master of the World!" (1) An apparent, but not serious, appeal to God to witness something remarkable; used as one would use "Holy Moses!" (2) An appeal to God to get through a difficult time, used like "God willing!"

Rosh Hashanah (H), *Rosh Hashone* (Y) Head of the year, i.e., the Jewish New Year, which comes in the early fall, on the first day of the month of Tishrei

schav, stschav (Y) Sorrel soup

schlemiel (Y) A misfit, a born loser

schnorrer (Y) A beggar, a moocher; a cheapskate, a chiseler

Sephardic (H) Jews from Iberia (Spain = Sepharad) and their descendents; all Jews who are not from Eastern or Western Europe; Jews who speak Judeo-Spanish (Ladino)

Shabbatai Zevi (H) Seventeenth-century false messiah from Turkey

Shammai (BCE 50–CE 30) Palestinian rabbi and contemporary of Hillel. Shammai's interpretations of the Law were known for their severity.

shmaltz (Y) Chicken fat

shmeer (Y) Spread, smear

shofar (H) Ram's horn, sounded on Rosh Hashanah and at the conclusion of Yom Kippur

shul (Y) Synagogue; school

smetene (Y) Sour cream

Tashlikh (H) The custom of symbolically casting one's sins into a moving body of water on the first afternoon of Rosh Hashanah, New Year's Day

tchatchke (Y) A toy or a trinket

teyglekh (Y) Sweet, honeyed pastries served especially at the New Year

Tishrei The seventh month of the Jewish calendar. The Jewish penitential period begins on the first day of Tishrei, with Rosh Hashanah, and extends ten days until Yom Kippur, the Day of Atonement.

traife, traif (H) Not kosher; food not permitted to Jews

Tsaytshrift far Purimdiker Fizik (Y) Fictitious name: *Journal of Physics for Purim*

tsimmis (Y) Mixed cooked vegetables and fruits; a big fuss

tzibbile (Y) Onion; *tzibbile bundehs*, onion rolls

ver veys (Y) Who knows?

yarmulke (Y) Skullcap worn by observant Jewish males; also called a *kipah* (H)

Yom Kippur (H) Day of Atonement

Zayde (Y) Grandfather

CONTRIBUTORS

ISAAC ABELLA, 1996, Department of Physics, University of Chicago. Currently professor in the same department.

HOWARD ARONSON, 1976, Departments of Slavic Languages and Literatures and of Linguistics, University of Chicago, where he is currently professor emeritus in those departments and on the Committee on Jewish Studies.

ALLAN BLOOM, 1981, Committee on Social Thought and the College, University of Chicago. At the time of his death in 1992, he was codirector of the John M. Olin Center for Inquiry into the Theory and Practice of Democracy, University of Chicago.

LEON CARNOVSKY, 1961, Graduate Library School, University of Chicago. Carnovsky remained a professor in the Library School until his retirement. He died in 1975.

MORREL H. COHEN, 1967, Department of Physics, University of Chicago. Currently on the research faculty of the Department of Astronomy and Physics at Rutgers.

STEPHEN Z. COHEN, 1975, Jane Addams School of Social Work, University of Illinois. Since his retirement, Cohen has been lecturing at the School of Social Service Administration, University of Chicago.

TED COHEN, 1976, Department of Philosophy, University of Chicago. Cohen is currently professor in the Department of Philosophy, the Committees on Art and Design and Interdisciplinary Studies in the Humanities, and the College, University of Chicago.

BERNARD S. COHN, 1968, Departments of History and Anthropology, University of Chicago. Cohn was professor emeritus when he retired in 1995; he died in 2003.

PETER F. DEMBOWSKI, 1975, Department of Romance Languages and Literatures, University of Chicago. Currently Distinguished Service Professor Emeritus of French in the Departments of Romance Languages and Literatures and Linguistics, the Committee on Medieval Studies, and the College, University of Chicago.

HASIA DINER, 1995, Department of History, University of Maryland. Currently, she is the Paul and Sylvia Steinberg Professor of American Jewish History in the Skirball Department of Hebrew and Judaic Studies of New York University.

WENDY DONIGER, 1999 (1991/1980), Divinity School, Department of South Asian Languages and Civilizations, University of Chicago. Doniger currently is the Mircea Eliade Distinguished Service Professor in the Divinity School, the Department of South Asian Languages and Civilizations, the Committees on the Ancient Mediterranean World and Social Thought, and the College, University of Chicago.

JACOB J. FELDMAN, 1959, Department of Sociology, University of Chicago. Feldman is senior fellow of the National Opinion Research Center, Bethesda, Maryland.

MILTON FRIEDMAN, 1963, Department of Economics, University of Chicago. Friedman is the Paul Snowden Russell Distinguished Service Professor Emeritus in the Department of Economics, University of Chicago, and has been senior research fellow at the Hoover Institution since 1977. Received the Nobel Prize in Economic Sciences in 1976.

GODFREY S. GETZ, 1986, Departments of Pathology and of Biochemistry and Molecular Biology, University of Chicago. Now the Donald N. Pritzker Distinguished Service Professor in those departments and the College, University of Chicago.

JACOB GETZELS, 1962, Departments of Education and Psychology, University of Chicago. At the time of his death in 2001, he was the R. Wendell Harrison Distinguished Service Professor in those departments.

ALAN GEWIRTH, 1983, Department of Philosophy, University of Chicago. At the time of his death in 2004, he was the Edward Carson Waller Distinguished Service Professor Emeritus, Department of Philosophy, University of Chicago.

EUGENE GOODHEART, 1964, Department of English, University of Chicago. Now professor emeritus in the Department of English and American Literature at Brandeis University.

PHILIP GOSSETT, 1977, Department of Music, University of Chicago. Currently the Robert W. Reneker Distinguished Service Professor in the Department of Music and the College, University of Chicago.

HANNA HOLBORN GRAY, 1991, president, University of Chicago; professor, Department of History. Currently president emerita and Harry Pratt Judson Distinguished Service Professor Emeritus in the Department of History and the College, University of Chicago.

HARRY HAROOTUNIAN, 1979, Departments of History and Far Eastern Languages and Civilizations, University of Chicago. Currently Max Palevsky Professor Emeritus in History, University of Chicago.

SIMON HELLERSTEIN, 1968, Department of Mathematics, University of Wisconsin. Retired in 2000 as professor in the same department.

ISRAEL N. HERSTEIN, 1972, Department of Mathematics, University of Chicago/Weitzman Institute of Sciences and Technology. On his death in 1988, he was professor in the Department of Mathematics, University of Chicago.

HARRY KALVEN, JR., 1961, University of Chicago Law School. Kalven remained professor in the Law School until his death in 1974.

ELIHU KATZ, 1958, 1959, Department of Sociology and the College, University of Chicago. Currently trustee professor of communication, Annenberg School for Communication, University of Pennsylvania, and professor emeritus of sociology and communication, the Hebrew University of Jerusalem.

HERBERT C. KELMAN, 1968, Department of Psychology, University of Michigan. After serving from 1993 to 2003 as director of the Program on International Conflict Analysis and Resolution at the Weatherhead Center for International Affairs, he is currently Richard Clarke Cabot Professor of Social Ethics, Emeritus, Department of Psychology, Harvard University.

ROBERT KIRSCHNER, 1981, Department of Pathology, University of Chicago Medical School. On his death in 2002 he was clinical associate in the Department of Pathology and Pediatrics, University of Chicago Medical School.

EDWARD W. KOLB, 1992, Department of Physics, University of Chicago. Currently professor in the Department of Astronomy and

Astrophysics, the Enrico Fermi Institute, and the College, University of Chicago.

JOHN D. LANTOS, 1993, Department of Pediatric Medicine, University of Chicago Medical School. Currently professor and section chief of general pediatrics, Departments of Pediatrics and Medicine, University of Chicago Medical School.

RICHARD LASHOF, 1974, Department of Mathematics, University of Chicago. Currently professor emeritus.

JOHN LASTER, 2003, estate planner, presented at George Washington University.

LEON M. LEDERMAN, 1990, Department of Physics, University of Chicago. Currently Frank L. Sulzberger Professor Emeritus in the Department of Physics, the Enrico Fermi Institute, and the College, University of Chicago, as well as resident scholar at the Illinois Mathematics and Science Academy. Received the 1988 Nobel Prize in Physics.

ROBIN LEIDNER, 1994, Department of Sociology, University of Pennsylvania. Currently associate professor and undergraduate chair there.

MURRAY H. LOEW, 2002, Department of Electrical and Computer Engineering, George Washington University.

DAVID MALAMENT, 1979, Department of Philosophy, University of Chicago. Currently Distinguished Professor of Logic and Philosophy of Science, Department of Philosophy, University of California, Irvine.

WILLIAM MEADOW, 1999, Department of Pediatrics, University of Chicago Medical School. Currently professor of neonatology in the Department of Pediatrics, University of Chicago Medical School.

FRANÇOISE MELTZER, 1986, Department of Comparative Literature, University of Chicago. Currently Mabel Greene Myers Professor in the Departments of Comparative Literature, Romance Languages and Literatures, the Divinity School, and the College, University of Chicago.

MARVIN MIRSKY, 1967, 1972, Humanities Collegiate Division, University of Chicago. Currently senior lecturer emeritus in the College, University of Chicago.

W. J. T. (TOM) MITCHELL, 1999, Departments of English Language and Literature and Art History, University of Chicago. Currently

Gaylord Donnelley Distinguished Service Professor in the Departments of English Language and Literature and Art History, the Committee on Art and Design, and the College, University of Chicago.

RALPH W. NICHOLAS, 1984, Department of Anthropology, University of Chicago. Currently William Rainey Harper Professor Emeritus in the Department of Anthropology and the College, University of Chicago.

MARTHA C. NUSSBAUM, 1997, Law School, Department of Philosophy, Divinity School, and the College, University of Chicago. Currently Ernst Freund Distinguished Service Professor in Law and Ethics, University of Chicago Law School.

EMILIE S. PASSOW, 1990, Department of English Literature, Swarthmore University. Currently adjunct professor in the Judaic Studies Program, Drexel University, she also leads a seminar on medical humanities at Thomas Jefferson Medical University.

JERROLD M. SADOCK, 1974, Department of Linguistics, University of Chicago. Currently Glen A. Lloyd Distinguished Service Professor in that department.

SHALOM SCHWARTZ, 1968, Department of Sociology, University of Wisconsin. Retired as professor from the Department of Psychology of the Hebrew University of Jerusalem.

HAROLD T. SHAPIRO, 1997, president, Princeton University. Currently president emeritus and professor of economics and public affairs, Department of Economics and the Woodrow Wilson School, Princeton University.

JUDITH SHAPIRO, 1990, Department of Anthropology, Bryn Mawr College. Currently president, Barnard College.

LAWRENCE SHERMAN, 1965, Department of Medicine, University of Wisconsin.

BERNARD S. SILBERMAN, 1979, Departments of Political Science and Far Eastern Studies, University of Chicago. Currently professor in the Department of Political Science and the College and a member of the Center for East Asian Studies, University of Chicago.

MICHAEL SILVERSTEIN, 1984, Department of Anthropology, University of Chicago. Currently Charles F. Grey Distinguished Service Professor in the Departments of Anthropology, Linguistics, and Psy-

chology and on the Committee on Interdisciplinary Studies in the
Humanities, University of Chicago.

BARBARA MARIA STAFFORD, 1994, Department of Art History, University of Chicago. Currently William B. Ogden Distinguished Service Professor in the Department of Art History and the College,
University of Chicago.

EDWARD STANKIEWICZ, 1966, Department of Linguistics, University
of Chicago. Now professor emeritus in the Department of Slavic
Languages and Literatures, Yale University.

NANCY L. STEIN, 1989, Departments of Psychology and Education,
University of Chicago. Currently professor in the Department of
Psychology, the Committee on Human Development, and the Col-
lege, University of Chicago.

JOSEF STERN, 1994, Department of Philosophy, University of
Chicago. Currently professor in the Department of Philosophy and
the College, University of Chicago.

GEOFFREY R. STONE, 1993, dean, University of Chicago Law School.
Currently Harry Kalven, Jr., Distinguished Service Professor in the
Law School and the College, University of Chicago.

STUART TAVE, 1982, Department of English, University of Chicago.
Currently William Rainey Harper Professor Emeritus in the College
and professor in the Department of English, University of Chicago.

SOL TAX, 1963, Department of Anthropology, University of Chicago.
On his death In 1995, he was professor emeritus in that department.

STEVEN WATTER, 1991, senior associate dean of the College and dean
of student life, Haverford College. That is his current position.

HAROLD WECHSLER, 1978, Department of Education, University of
Chicago. Currently professor of educational leadership, Margaret
Warner Graduate School of Education and Human Development,
University of Rochester.

BERNARD A. WEISBERGER, 1961, Department of History, University
of Chicago. Also taught at Wayne State University and the University of Rochester before devoting himself full time to writing.

MARIAMNE H. WHATLEY, 1983, School of Education, University of
Wisconsin. Currently chair of the Women's Studies Program, professor of curriculum and instruction, and associate dean, School of Education, University of Wisconsin.

PAUL ROOT WOLPE, 1999, Department of Sociology, University of Pennsylvania. Currently professor in the Department of Psychiatry, University of Pennsylvania, where he also holds appointments in the Departments of Medical Ethics and Sociology and is senior fellow in Penn's Center for Bioethics. He is also chief of bioethics for NASA.

JUDITH ZEITLIN, 1998, Department of East Asian Languages and Civilizations, University of Chicago. Currently professor in that department.